RIDING THE CREST OF THE WAVES

DARING TO BELIEVE
WHAT WE BELIEVE

Russell G. Ruffino

For those who believe

For those who used to believe

For those who want to believe

For those who wonder about believing

For those who don't know what to believe

Table of Contents

Preface

If you are looking for academic arguments and biblical scholar-ship with explanatory footnotes and a bibliography of resourc-es and references, these essays are not for you. What you will find in these pages is just the fruit of a lot of years of personal study and experience in very simple language. I expect that many will strongly disagree with what I offer. Some may easily dismiss it all. Some may even mock what I say.

On the other hand, over the years people have reacted posi-tively to the kind of thinking these essays represent. People have been turned on by this kind of thinking. They were grate-ful, and encouraged me to write. I hope that these essays will be helpful to those who believe—or used to believe—or want to believe—or wonder about believing—or don't know what to believe, but find it impossible to buy what Christianity—the church—advertises. I hope also that maybe, just maybe, the ideas I offer in these essays can help move forward the thinking offered by others with arguments and scholarship—the kind of thinking that will blossom at last into the gift to people, to the human story and to the world that the Christian faith is truly meant to be.

I have been at this for a long time—preaching, teaching and hoping, always hoping, that Christianity—the church in all its denominations—will begin to grow into what it is truly meant to be. I know I am far from alone in this hope, but I confess that I can feel quite alone and even without hope. Like others who hope for a revolution in the Spirit, I feel as if I were standing on the seashore and trying to turn back the waves of the sea and all I have in my hand is a teaspoon. Then, despite my desperation, I see that we who live in hope are the ones *riding the crest of the waves*, and there on the shore are those who represent the past and the status quo, and they are the ones wielding their spoons. Our growth in the Spirit cannot be stopped. Many of us will not live to see the full enlightenment to come, but we see flashes of the Light, and we can all believe, believe with everything that is in us, that it is coming.

There's a familiar passage in Isaiah 11:6-7—a Christmas-time passage—and the pictures Isaiah offers are popular themes for Christmas cards. The wolf will live with the lamb. The leopard will lie down with young goats. The calf and the lion together. Little children as leaders. The cow and the bear grazing together. The lion eating straw like an ox. For a lion a calf is lunch. Children as leaders? Bears eating grass? A bear would much more enjoy the cow. Lions eating straw? The ox would be more to their taste. Fantastic pictures!

To be Christian means to commit ourselves to things that never were—to commit ourselves to fantastic things. To be Christian means to believe in the one who proclaims, "See, I am making all things new." A new freedom. New hearts. A new way of thinking. New priorities. A new way of living. A new kind of justice. A new kind of service. A new kind of peace. A new way of forgiving. A new way of loving. A new kind of leadership. New life. A new world. To be Christian means to believe in topsy-turvy change and that what is being made new are the building blocks of a divine-human-cosmic reality.

There are too many who do not understand that what is to come, or what Christians are called to believe in, or what Christians are supposed to make happen, is fantastic. They do not recognize what is already happening. There are too many church leaders and too many politicians who have come to believe that by holding back the future they are doing the very will of God. No one can hold back the future. No one can hold back the fantastic things that are coming and are already here. No one can hold back the Spirit of God. He is at work, and the psalmist says "He whose throne is in heaven is laughing" (Psalm 2:4), laughing at their comedy. To be Christian means to believe in what is indeed fantastic—to believe in the Spirit with his fire who fills all things, calling all of us to look always beyond what has been and what is to what never was. We have to dare to believe what we believe.

I pray that the God of our Lord Jesus Christ ...may give you a spirit of wisdom and revelation as you come to know him, so that, with the eyes of your heart enlightened, you may know what is the hope to which he has called you, what are the riches of his glorious inheritance... and what is the immeasurable greatness of his power for us who believe, according to the workings of his great power. (Ephesians 1: 17-18)

"Here I Am, Lord"

First let me tell you my story.

I'm a New Jersey native. I lived in Massachusetts and Rhode Island for thirty-five years, so I consider myself a New Englander. Rooting for the Boston Red Sox is part of my religion. My wife, Barbara, is a Washington, DC native. I met her in DC, and we began our life together there. We've called several places home, and now we are back in DC. We don't expect to be doing any more moving around, at least not as far and wide as we have been doing. Let me back up, but not too far.

After my graduation from Seton Hall University in New Jersey (then still Seton Hall College), the next step in my training for priesthood in the Roman Catholic Church would have been four years of theology at the local seminary thirty miles north in Mahwah, a Native American name that roughly translates as "Where the hell are we." Instead I was sent to do my four years of theology at the Pontifical Gregorian University in Rome. More than sixty nations were represented at the "Greg" among the students and the faculty. Our common language was Latin, and while the social life of the university was conducted in Italian, the lectures, the textbooks and the exams were in Latin. It took about three months, but I actually started thinking in Latin! My experience at the Greg with the Jesuits opened my mind and my heart in ways I could never have imagined—nothing like that could have happened in Mahwah. In keeping with their world-wide reputation the Jesuit professors were first-class educators, and more than anything else they taught us how to think for ourselves. Later on I looked back at these Jesuits as "Anglicans." I completed my theological studies and received a licentiate in sacred theology (STL), a degree that qualified me to teach theology. I was ordained a priest in the chapel of the American residence, the North American College on the Janiculum Hill.

I returned to the States expecting a parish assignment, but instead I was asked to return to Rome and the Greg to pursue a doctorate in philosophy. That was another four year program; I focused on philosophical and theological issues related to the sciences. I was eager to get to work back home, so I put it together in three years. With the PhD I began teaching philosophy in the School of Divinity of Seton Hall, not on its main campus, but in Mahwah, and on weekends I helped out at a nearby parish. What I especially enjoyed were the opportunities I had to lecture on college campuses and preach in churches throughout the state, and to become involved in regional and national ecumenical activities. In 1967 I was invited to teach at the Catholic University of America in Washington, DC as an assistant professor, eventually realizing that I was living a kind of double life, teaching and preaching as the Roman Catholic Church expected, but my mind and heart were not in it. The encyclical of Pope Paul VI condemning all forms of "artificial" birth control became the catalyst that finally moved me to take off the collar and walk away.

I got a job in the US Office of Education right there in DC. Six months later I met Barbara Casey. Three weeks after that I asked her to marry me, and she said yes! A very good friend, an Episcopal priest I came to know in New Jersey, officiated at our wedding—a sign of things to come. Mike was born the following year. When we felt we had had enough of Washington, I asked for a reassignment to the regional office in Boston. The town and New England felt like our natural habitat. We bought a house in the suburbs, and the following year Jane was born. I was appointed assistant regional commissioner for higher education for New England, and after well over a decade in the regional office I took the position of academic dean at one of the Boston colleges.

In the meantime I found myself attending as often as I could the weekday noon service at the cathedral of the Episcopal Diocese of Massachusetts. The Spirit was hard at work. The details of how our journey went, I think, are downright fascinating and rather mysterious, but it's enough to say that Barb, Mike, Jane and I were received as members of the Episcopal Church in 1988. Then I went bishop shopping.

I found that the bishop of the Episcopal Diocese of Rhode Island was the kind of shepherd I wanted to serve with, and in 1990 he received me as a priest in the Episcopal Church. After serving a variety of temporary, part-time parish assignments, in 1991 I was called as vicar of the Church of Saint Peter's-by-the-Sea, in the town of Narragansett, and I took on the challenge of serving the people of "South County". The bishop added a couple of diocesan jobs, such as chairing the Committee for Continuing Education of the Clergy. The motto and goal of Saint Peter's, emblazoned on our parish banner, was "to make our embrace as wide as God's,"—and we provided service and assistance to everyone who came to us, members and nonmembers, Episcopalians and people of other traditions, and even those from no religious tradition at all. This open-door policy resulted not only in tripling the size of the congregation and quadrupling the number of children in our Sunday school, but we also believed it gave people a very positive attitude about the church and about religion. On

Easter Sunday, 2007, I laid down that calling and looked forward to what retirement might bring.

In the spring of 2008, the rector of Saint Paul's Episcopal Church in Rome telephoned me to ask if I might be interested in serving as vicar of a mission in Orvieto, a town about an hour's train ride north of Rome. After Barb said, "Why not?," I was once more off to Italy. I gave the mission almost four years, and then in 2012 I returned to the States—not to New England, but to join Barb once again in Washington.

More than anything else, I have loved teaching and preaching. I love doing what I can to see lights go on in people's faces. I love doing what I can to open people's minds and to free up their thinking about God and them and them and God and their relationships with one another. That is what moved me to write these essays and to tell a few stories.

Now what?

Here I am, Lord.

Thank you

William Temple, Archbishop of
Canterbury, 1942—1944

Pierre Teilhard de Chardin, the
prophet, 1881—1955

John Shelby Spong, Episcopal
Bishop of Newark, New Jersey,
1979—2000

Who provided light for me
To see the Christian Faith and all
religious faith in a new way
To see the world and the whole of
evolving creation in a new way
To see who we are in a new way
To see what really matters

Barbara, who put up with me all
these years,
for her brilliant encouragement

Mike and Jane,
my best contribution
to the enterprise

Introduction

Christianity needs to do the kind of rethinking that will make any other reform look like a Sunday afternoon walk in the park. Christianity needs to be fundamentally redefined—refocused. Actually, Christianity is not meant to be defined. It is meant to be lived, but from the very beginning Christianity lost its way. Again and again it took wrong turns. People didn't get what Christianity is really all about. I think most of us still don't get it. Mahatma Gandhi was asked once whether he thought Christianity had failed. "It hasn't yet been tried," he answered. I think he was right.

There are three principles that should guide our rethinking—to get at what Christianity is all about:

1. We should make our embrace as wide as God's.

Christianity always has to put people first and reach out to everybody—no exceptions. People come first—as they are, as they really are. People come first. The individual always comes first. People's relationship with God, their relationship with one another, their hopes, needs, problems, challenges, happiness, peace—always first. Nothing comes before

people—nothing—not creeds and traditions, not law and order, not church rules and practices, not even the Bible. Nothing
comes before people.

> I sought to hear the voice of God,
> And climbed the highest steeple;
> But God declared, "Go down again";
> I dwell among the people.
> (From Louis I. Newman,
> 1893—1972, "The Voice of God")

2. Some see things as they are, and ask why; let's dream
of things that never were and ask why not.

This line, written by George Bernard Shaw in *Back to
Methuselah,* was later paraphrased by Robert F. Kennedy.
Christianity has to be wide open to the Spirit of God—wide-
open to possibilities—wide-open to things that continually
surprise us—to things that may even shock us. Christianity has
to live and move and have its being in faith—faith in universal
evolution—in the divine-human-cosmic enterprise—faith that
the forward movement of the enterprise is in our hands—faith
that the future of the world and the coming of the realm of God
are one and the same enterprise, moved and empowered by one
and the same Spirit.

3. You have not touched the truth until a thousand sincere people have denounced you for blasphemy.

This is a statement made by Anthony Campolo of Eastern
University. Christianity has to be bold, courageous, and fearless in pursuing what is true and what is good. The true and
the good partake of the infinity of God. Christianity, like all

religion, has to confess that it diminishes God—that it wants a God of manageable size, who fits its stories, expectations, structures, doctrines and morality. Christianity says "infinite" God, and in spite of itself, it limits God to this planet or maybe to our solar system, or limits God to expanses of time it can get its mind around. Christianity has to confess it has wanted an infinite God who is finite. Christianity has to think like science. Nothing is beyond question. Nothing is that *sacred*.

Let me tell you a story. This story, like the other stories I share with you, has nothing to do with anything. It's just a story I think you'll enjoy.

This happened while I was a student priest at the North American College in Rome, ordained, but not yet finished with my theological studies at the Greg. It was Easter time, and as was the custom, pastors throughout the city were busy visiting and blessing the homes of their people. The pastors needed help; there were just too many homes to cover. Some of the pastors contacted student priests' residences like our college to ask for help. I reported to Saint Mark's Church in the Piazza Venezia, the very heart of the city. The pastor sat at a table in the parish hall, assigning areas of the parish to the priests who came to help. He gave me an area of small apartment buildings near the Victor Emmanuel Monument. He also assigned each of us an altar boy, who could help us find our way and carry the vessel of holy water.

At all the apartments I visited the families welcomed me warmly and were grateful for the visit and the blessing. Toward the end of the day I came to what appeared to be a particularly large apartment on the top floor of one of the buildings. The young woman who answered the door was especially delighted with my offer to bless the apartment; she was downright excited. Dressed in a housecoat, she led me through the apartment. Several other young women appeared, also dressed in housecoats. In the blessing of a home there is a specific prayer for each of the rooms, but in this apartment there was no living room, no dining room, no family room—only bedrooms. I followed the woman, with the other women in procession behind us, from bedroom to bedroom, saying the same prayer in each. It struck me that the altar boy, who was eleven or twelve years old, looked as if he was trying hard not to burst out laughing.

When I finished, the women gathered around me and gushed with their appreciation. I left the apartment, and the women came out to the stairwell. As I went down the stairs, I overheard one woman, leaning over the railing, say to the others, "Come bellino"—"How cute". It was only years later, (after I had left the ministry in the Roman Catholic Church and was married) that in telling the story to a group of friends—kidding my wife Barbara about how those women thought I was "cute"—what I had done dawned on me. It was no wonder that the altar boy struggled not to laugh; he must have had a good laugh with his buddies later. In light of my visit maybe those women not only assured their clients of their good health, as women in that oldest of professions were legally required to do, but they could also advertise that their "house" was approved by the Vatican—or as businesses are eager to claim, that theirs was a purveyor to the Holy See!

We Made Some Wrong Turns

Christianity made wrong turns, which darkened its message and frustrated its mission.

- Christianity cut itself off from its Jewish roots. Anti-Semitism became part of the thinking and life of the church. More fundamentally, instead of interpreting the Bible as its Jewish writers intended, the church took the words of the Bible quite literally.
- The church chose to understand human nature and the world *negatively*—in terms that were downright platonic and not at all Judeo-Christian. The material body was seen as the prison of the spiritual soul, the body as only the instrument of the mind and the soul, the world as merely a stage to strut upon, and death as the soul's release from the body and the world.
- Christianity took on the trappings of the Roman Empire and became an institution that could ensure unity, order, discipline and control.
- The leaders of the church—the clergy—were raised above the people. A sacred ritual was set up—ordination, which *conferred* spiritual power that only the ordained could validly exercise.

- The church's teachings about women degraded them, denied them their   dignity and excluded them from their rightful role in the life of the church and in society.
- The church claimed exclusive, infallible and universal authority to teach what is true and what is right. To be a faithful Christian required internal acknowledgement of the church's intellectual authority. The Christian way, rather primarily, became something of the mind—something about how a person thinks.
- In its missionary endeavor the church disregarded, disrespected, and even destroyed the culture of peoples everywhere.
- The church deliberately and forcefully took stands against democracy, freedom of conscience, and the progress of science, human knowledge and discovery.

A Prayer for Our Church

No, no; religion is a spring
That from some secret, golden mine
Derives her birth, and thence doth bring
Cordials in every drop, and wine.

But in her long and hidden course
Passing through the earth's dark veins,
Grows still from better unto worse,
And both her taste and color stains.

Heal then these waters, Lord; or bring thy flock,
Since these are troubled, to thy springing rock;
Look down, Great Master of the feast, O shine,
And turn once more our water into wine.
                              (Henry Vaughn, 1622-1695)

It's Time to Let Go

In light of the advances in science and in our understanding of the human story, there are conclusions Christians cannot escape.

- There were no Adam and Eve.
- There was no Garden of Eden—no paradise to be lost.
- There was no original sin.
- There was no need for the bloody sacrifice of a divine person to set things right between the human race and God.
- We do not come into this world personally guilty of sin.
- Jesus of Nazareth was not born of a virgin.
- This Jesus did not offer himself to torture and execution in vicarious punishment for an original sin never committed by individuals who never existed, or for our sins.
- The raising of Jesus from death does not mean the resuscitation of his corpse.
- Jesus did not ascend bodily into the sky.
- Jesus did not establish a hierarchical organization with divine, and surely not infallible, authority.

What is the Faith really all about? What does being a Christian mean? What does Christianity have to tell the world? What is the point of the Jesus story? Is there a point to the Jesus story that is embedded in our real world?

The Faith.

Billions of years ago evolution got under way, and finally we human beings appeared on the scene. Evolution and the coming of the realm of God are one enterprise. The enterprise is in our hands. This is our challenge. The answer to those questions about the Faith is simply this: *we are not alone.* In facing this challenge we are not alone. It is time for Christianity to reinterpret its myths and legends and its symbols, teachings and traditions, fundamentally and completely. It's time—and more than time—for Christianity to refocus.

The focus of the Faith: the very life and power of the infinite God dwell within us and among us. In this life and power we can overcome whatever stands in our way; we can overcome whatever is in ourselves and in our world that holds us back. In this life and power together we can do all things. We are partners with God in the divine-human-cosmic enterprise to know and understand ourselves, to know and understand this earth and indeed the whole universe. It is an enterprise in which we are called and empowered to heal and to create—to make all things new.

Faith is about belief in ourselves. Faith is about belief in this enterprise. Faith is about belief in this life and power that raises us and all things to heights and possibilities we can hardly begin to imagine. The raising of the man Jesus from death is the pivotal event of all time because it reveals the overall significance and the power that is present and at work in the evolutionary process since the beginning of time.

Faith is not about the mind's acceptance of doctrines and definitions. Faith is the aspiration of the heart. Faith is belief in a vision that is always beyond us, drawing us. Faith leads us and inspires us to ask questions—the questions that matter in the divine-human-cosmic enterprise. To question is part of the definition of faith. To question is to worship. We have only just begun to understand ourselves and this cosmos. We have only just begun to understand what is true and what is right. We have only just begun to understand where we are going. The divine-human-cosmic enterprise has only just begun. Faith is essentially involved in the material things of this awesome universe. Faith calls us to live, work and serve with the conviction that material things and the stuff of our lives are the building blocks of an everlasting reality that we, as partners with God, have only just begun to build. Faith reveals to us that the life and power—the energy—in which we face the challenge of this enterprise has a Name—Total and Unconditional Love.

It is time to let go of the myths, legends, symbols, teachings and traditions of our religious childhood, and know them for what they are—the human attempts to package what the Faith is really all about.

This is what Christianity has to tell the world—to inspire the world to accept this challenge, and to assure the world that we are not alone in meeting this challenge. Surely, but slowly, this was revealed in the human story from its very beginning. It became clearer as time went on. This is what has become abundantly clear—uniquely clear—in the Jesus story.

Let me tell you a story, and this story is about the enterprise.

Partners

Before there was anything, there was God, a few angels, and a huge swirling glob of rocks and water with no place to go. The angels asked God, "Why don't you clean up this mess?"

So God collected rocks from the huge swirling glob and put them together in clumps and said, "Some of these clumps of rocks will be planets, and some will be stars, and some of these rocks will be…just rocks."

Then God collected water from the huge swirling glob and put it together in pools of water and said, "Some of these pools of water will be oceans, and some will be clouds, and some of this water will be…just water."

Then the angels said, "Well, God, it's neater now, but is it finished?"

"NOPE!"

On some of the rocks God placed growing things, and creeping things, and things that only God knows what they are, and when God had done all this, the angels asked God, "Is it finished now?" And God answered,

"NOPE!"

God made a man and a woman from some of the water and dust and said to them, "I am tired now. Please finish up the world for me." But the man and woman said, "We can't finish the world alone! You have the plans and we are too little. "

"You are big enough," God answered them. "But I agree to this. If you keep trying to finish the world, I will be your partner."

The man and the woman asked, "What's a partner?" and God answered, "A partner is someone you work with on a big thing that neither of you can do alone. If you have a partner, it means that you can never give up, because your partner is depending on you. On the days you think I am not doing enough and on the days I think you are not doing enough, even on those days we are still partners and we must not stop trying to finish the world. That's the deal." And they all agreed to that deal.

Then the angels asked God, "Is the world finished yet?" and God answered, "I don't know. Go ask my partners."

(From **Does God Have a Big Toe?** *by Marc Gellman and Oscar de Mejo; pp. 1—3)*

God Didn't Dictate the Bible

Is God himself the author of the Bible? Are the words of the writers of the books of the Bible actually God's words? Answer: God is not the author of the Bible. If there is something sacred about the Scriptures, it is not because God is their author. It's because of people's effort to describe their experience of God that we find in them. What we find in the Bible might be true or untrue, right or wrong, accurate or inaccurate, reasonable or outrageous, or even downright silly. What matters is the God-experience that moved the writers to want to tell others about it. What matters is whether their God-experiences touch us in some way. That makes the Scriptures sacred.

Interpreting the words of the Bible as authoritative in themselves has led to some terrible beliefs—e.g., that owning slaves, or slaughtering your enemies, or physically abusing women and children, or restricting and denying freedom of conscience are morally acceptable.

The words of the Bible are used to judge our neighbor, to hold back the advance of science, and to make people afraid. How could such words be God's words? Those who wrote the Jewish scriptures, the Old Testament, believed in their God-experience, and tried to describe it, using whatever knowledge, concepts and language they had. People who knew Jesus of

Nazareth believed that in him they experienced God in a new way, and they wrote about their experience in the Christian scriptures, the New Testament, using whatever knowledge, concepts and language they had.

For centuries all this shared God-experience has touched people. The Bible can help us—can inspire us—to connect with God and connect better with one another, but to believe that God himself is the author of the Bible and so claim that the words of the Bible have divine authority in themselves leads to deliberate blindness, and much pain, division and un-love, and even to hate and violence. Most of all, such a belief about this Book holds us back from becoming everything we are called by God to be for ourselves, for one another, for the world and for the coming of the realm of God.

There Were No Adam and Eve

The story of Adam and Eve goes like this. This perfect first man and perfect first woman, the parents of the whole human race, lived in a perfect relationship with God in a perfect kind of life in an earthly paradise in a perfect world that had all come complete and finished from the hand of God. Adam and Eve disobeyed God, and because of their disobedience they lost their relationship with God, and lost their perfect life and their perfect world not only for themselves, but for the whole human race. Christianity has taught that every person who comes into this world inherits their sin—the original sin.

Science gives us a very—very—different story. Millions of years ago one branch of life in its evolution split into two sub-branches. One of these developed into apes and the other developed into human beings. This happened in a variety of places on earth and at different points in time. These humans were not perfect; they were brutish. Life for them was far from being any kind of paradise. The world was not complete and finished. Everything, including humans, evolved and contin-ued to evolve. Any idea about gods came much later. These first humans had to struggle for survival, but hardly as the result of some human disobedience. The human race has come a long way since its beginnings, and the challenge continues.

No "Adam and Eve" and no "original sin" with all its "consequences" means that Christianity has to rethink its teachings about who we human beings are and who Jesus of Nazareth was. For one thing—and nothing could be more fundamental—Jesus did not suffer and die on the cross in vicarious expiation for an original sin never committed by first parents who never existed or for our sins.

Our human nature is not corrupt; it is not in rebellion against God. Our human nature is incomplete. We are not fallen. We are in process. We did not need and do not need to be restored to what never was. We are empowered by the Spirit of God, the same Spirit who was in Jesus the Christ, to become what we should be and will be for ourselves, for others, for the world and for the realm of God. God raises us to share in his very life and graces us with the privilege and the responsibility to cultivate the garden—his garden and our garden, ours and his. We cultivate the divine-human-cosmic garden that is not limited by the measurements of space and time—a garden that will blossom, and is already blossoming, into the eternal reality, when eons and eons and eons from now, beyond space and time, God will be all in all, and we and the whole of creation will be perfected in God.

There are Christians who believe in a doctrine called the Immaculate Conception of Mary, the mother of Jesus—that by a unique privilege she was conceived without the guilt of original sin, "our tainted nature's solitary boast." (From"The Virgin", by William Wordsworth, 1770—1850) The fact is, to be conceived untainted is neither unique nor a privilege. We are really all "immaculately conceived."

God Is Not Bloodthirsty

We have not been "redeemed", "saved"," healed" or "empowered" and things are not "made new" through the suffering and death of Jesus the Christ. God did not will nor require his suffering and death. Jesus of Nazareth was not born to suffer and to die. He was born to live as no one had ever lived and to love as no one had ever loved. The Christian Faith, its message and significance, are not centered in violence and blood. People are rightly put off by a bloodthirsty God. People are rightly put off by a God who demanded the sacrifice of an innocent man as the way the "human debt of disobedience could be paid"—by a God who nailed his son to a cross. People are rightly put off because Christians have believed , preached, taught, prayed and sung with thanksgiving that Jesus the Christ suffered and died for us—because Christians have believed, preached, taught, prayed and sung that as suffering and death were God's will for Jesus, so the suffering and death the world experiences can and even should be understood as God's will for us.

What should Christianity believe, preach, teach, pray and sing about Jesus the Christ? What is the meaning of the cross? What was God's will on Calvary? What *happened* on Calvary? Nothing happened on Calvary, but something eternal was once and for all revealed. God did not demand a blood sacrifice. Suffering and death are not of God, not for Jesus the Christ and not for the world. On Calvary the will of God was threefold. Firstly, to reveal the power of God, the divine power whose Name is Love and who overcomes all things, even death—to reveal the power in which all things are possible. Secondly, to reveal how far God's Love reaches; day after day in everything Jesus said and did the Love of God was revealed, until it was perfectly revealed on the cross. How far does the Love of God go? This far. Thirdly, to reveal how far our love for one another should reach. How far should people give of themselves for others? This far.

It is not through suffering and death—it is not through violence and blood—that we are "redeemed","saved","healed" or "empowered" and things are "made new". It is by infinitely powerful Love who is God. The cross does not mean to say to the world that God's will for Jesus the Christ was suffering and death, or that suffering and death could be God's will for us. The Cross is the locus and the sign of the victory of the loving power of God over suffering and death. The cross should not make the world recall that Jesus the Christ suffered and died on it. The cross proclaims that on it Jesus entered the life of God— that on it the Man Jesus began to live like God—and proclaims that all people and the whole of creation share in this power, in this Love, and in this Life. This was God's will for Jesus the Christ. This is God's will for us who share in the same Divine Spirit who dwelled in Jesus the Christ. God did not nail Jesus to the cross; soldiers did. God transformed this horror into the everlasting Light by which the world could know God's loving power and true will, first for Jesus the Christ, and then for us and for the world. We are "redeemed", "saved","healed" or "empowered", not through a bloody sacrifice, but by Divine Love, by the indwelling Spirit of God—by the Gift of the divine loving power for life, for which God demanded no payment.

Christianity did not begin in suffering and death—in violence and blood. It began in the overwhelming excitement of a band of Jewish men and women, who believed they experienced the infinite power of the Love of God in Jesus of Nazareth. It began in their joy that this Man who died, not by the will of God, but by execution by those who feared him, was gloriously alive. It began in their conviction that what Jesus had told them about the love of God, the power of love, and a new world was true, and that as death could not contain him, so death could not contain them. This is the Christian Faith—faith in our possibilities and in the world's possibilities here and now and into forever—possibilities in the power of Love, the Love, the Divine Spirit, perfectly revealed on the cross. The cross calls us and the world to believe in the power of love. The cross should inspire us and the whole world to follow Jesus's New Commandment to love even as he loved—not as if we love by our own power, but that we love by the power of the indwelling God whose Name is Love, and with whom all things are possible.

When Christians come to understand the true meaning of the cross, a lot of their preaching, most of their prayers, and particularly a great deal of what they sing will have to be put away.

In the ancient catacombs of Rome you can find symbols of the Good Shepherd, bread, the cup, the fish, but not the cross. Early Christians again and again heard the story of how Jesus suffered and died, but they thought of him not as the one who suffered and died. For them, Jesus was the one who is gloriously alive—the one who revealed that through love we become everything we are called to be for ourselves and for one another, and that through love the world is made new.

A modern-day parable from a book, **Rediscovering Religion,** *by J. S. Guleria*

It happened that a great virus swept the world over the course of a year. Everyone, regardless where they lived, was getting sick and dying. Doctors worked on an antidote around the clock. The whole world was in serious trouble. Finally, the virus' genetic code was broken. The doctors were confident a cure would follow quickly, but the antidote would require the blood of someone who had not been infected.

So, on every radio station and TV channel and Internet chat room the call went out. Everyone was to go to the nearest hospital to get blood taken for testing. The person or persons found without the virus would literally save the world. Weeks passed, and no one with uninfected blood was found. Hope sank. Then, a family from a small town went to a city hospital with a long line of people out the door. Nurses were coming out and pricking fingers and taking blood samples. Eventually the nurses got to the small family. After taking their blood, nurses told them and the others to wait in the parking lot, and when they heard the whistle, they could go home. So the family waited, scared, with their neighbors, wondering if this indeed was the end of the world.

Suddenly a nurse came running out of the hospital, screaming. She was yelling a name and waving a clipboard. The man's son tugged on his father's jacket, and said, "Daddy, that's me." The nurse grabbed the boy. His father protested, but she said, "It's OK; his blood is clean. Your son is the person the world has been looking for. We've got to get him away from infected people immediately." News spread fast. Soon radio and TV were broadcasting from the parking lot. People were laughing in joy and relief. It seemed like the first time anyone had heard laughing in a long time. Then a doctor appeared and pulled the man and his wife aside. "May we see you for a moment? We didn't realize that the donor might be a minor, and we need", the doctor choked up, and then finished, "we need you to sign a consent form." The couple began to sign and then the father saw the number of pints of blood to be taken from their only son had been left blank. "How many pints?," the father asked. The doctor bowed his head. "We had no idea the donor would be a little child. We weren't prepared. I'm sorry. We need it all." "But, but, you don't understand, this is our only son," the father explained. The doctor replied, "We are talking about the whole world here. Please sign." They did. Then the doctor said, "Would you like to have a moment with him?" In the room the child was sitting on an examining table. He saw his father first. "Daddy, what's going on? Did I do something wrong?" The father took his son's hand and said, "Your mommy and I love you, and we would never ever let anything happen to you that didn't just have to be. Do you understand?" Before the child could answer, the doctor came back in. "I'm sorry; we've got to get started."

What parent would sign such a consent form? Our God did. He gave his son up for us so that the world could live. "A child has been born for us, a son given to us."

Like this story, this modern parable, Christian teaching, Christian prayer and Christian hymns hasten to tell the world Jesus was born to suffer and die to redeem the world—to shed his most precious blood to save the world.

Christians everywhere may find this parable touching, beautiful and inspiring.

WRONG! It is horrible. It makes God a bloodthirsty God. Christians have some fundamental, radical rethinking to do about the cross and about what did and didn't happen on Calvary.

Jesus's Corpse Did Not Come Back to Life.

The Bible stories about the resurrection of Jesus go like this.

In the Gospel of Mark, the earliest of the four Gospels, a group of women goes to Jesus's tomb. When they arrive, they see that the stone that sealed the tomb has been rolled away. They see a young man dressed in white. He tells them Jesus has been raised. He instructs the women to tell Peter and the disciples that they will see Jesus in Galilee. The women flee in terror and amazement. They say nothing to anyone.

In the Gospel of Matthew, two women named Mary go to the tomb. As soon as they arrive, there is an earthquake. An angel appears and moves the stone from the tomb. The soldiers, who were guarding the tomb, see all this and they faint away. The angel tells the two Marys to go tell the disciples they will see Jesus in Galilee. With fear and joy the women go to tell the disciples what they saw and heard. On their way Jesus appears to the women, and he too tells them to tell the disciples they will see him in Galilee. When the disciples hear this news, they go to Galilee, where they see Jesus on a mountain.

In the Gospel of Luke, a group of women goes to the tomb. When they arrive, the stone at the entrance of the tomb has been rolled away. They go into the tomb. Two men appear. They tell the women Jesus has been raised, and say to them, "Remember this is what he told you when he was with you in Galilee." The women run to tell Peter and the disciples. Peter goes to the tomb, verifies that the body of Jesus is gone, and is amazed. Then the disciples see Jesus in and around Jerusalem.

In the Gospel of John, Mary Magdalene goes to the tomb alone. The stone has already been rolled away. She does not enter the tomb. She runs to tell Peter and the others that Jesus's body has been stolen. Peter and John run to the tomb, enter, and see that the body is gone. They return to where the others are gathered. Mary Magdalene remains at the tomb, and she sees Jesus. Then the disciples see Jesus in and around Jerusalem and in Galilee.

It's the most stupendous event in history and no one gets the story straight, and all those mentioned in the stories are supposed to be eye witnesses? Paul in his writings doesn't say anything about an empty tomb or all this coming and going, and everything he wrote was written before any of the Gospels.

Did you ever think about this? We read in the story of the resurrection in the Gospel of John: "Then Simon Peter...saw the linen wrappings lying there and the cloth that had been on Jesus's head, not lying with the linen wrappings, but rolled up in a place by itself." (John 20: 6-7) If we are to take the resurrection stories literally, and if we are to understand the resurrection of Jesus as a physical event—that is, if it means that his corpse was resuscitated, and he left the tomb—then in view of what Simon Peter saw, either Jesus walked out of the tomb naked, or he got some clothing somewhere. Surely, he wasn't naked when he spoke to Mary Magdalene and "the other Mary" (Matthew 28: 9-10), or when he spoke with Mary Magdalene alone (John 20: 16-17). So, where would Jesus have gotten his clothes?

Belief in the resurrection of Jesus is not based on the gospel stories, or on whether the stories can be untangled and the discrepancies resolved. Belief is founded in the experience to which these stories point—the experience the stories attempt to express. The point is that there would be no such stories unless people had an experience so indescribable that the stories became necessary to at least try to explain it.

To be in touch with that experience it is first of all essential to understand what the resurrection of Jesus was not. It does not mean that Jesus's corpse was resuscitated. It does not mean Jesus came back from death to the life he had known for some thirty years. It does not mean Jesus awakened, left the tomb and began walking around Judea and Galilee again. The resurrection of Jesus was a real event, but it was infinitely more than physical. The resurrection happened at a point in time and in a place, but it also happened beyond time and beyond any place. Jesus was raised among human beings and in God. The resurrection means that Jesus who died on the cross began to live like the eternal and infinite God. The disciples came to believe in the realm of God, a divine-human-cosmic reality of supernatural power, and from within this realm of God Jesus came to them gloriously alive.

The resurrection of Jesus reveals that the Spirit of God whose Name is Love is at work and has always been at work. Other events in the human story also reveal that God is at work, but the resurrection of Jesus confirms all other revelation. The resurrection confirms the belief that we are "redeemed"— "saved"— "healed" and "empowered"—and all things are being made new in the one and the same indwelling Spirit in whom Jesus was raised. The Christian Faith in the resurrection is not based on the biblical stories. Faith in the resurrection of Jesus is not about a physical event that happened in the distant past—a man coming back from the dead. The resurrection is the confirmation of the revelation of who we are, what we can be, what life can be. The resurrection is about what is happening today and what can happen tomorrow in the power of the Spirit of God. It confirms the view of a glorious future, the view not limited to what we can see and measure and count, but the view in which we are all sisters and brothers, partners with God, in a divine-human-cosmic enterprise that reaches into forever.

If Lazarus really came out of his tomb, according to the story in the Gospel of John (John 11:38—44), and if there had been cameras in those days, could the disciples have taken photos of the event? If it actually happened, then, yes, photos could have been taken of Lazarus hopping out of his tomb, and people unwinding the cloth he was wrapped in, and the look of amazement on the faces of all who witnessed the event.

When Jesus was raised from death, if someone were there with a camera, could that event have been photographed? No!

Artists have painted beautiful pictures of the resurrection of Jesus, but the fact is that our human minds, limited to physical space and time, cannot imagine it.

Jesus's physical ascension into heaven doesn't really make sense. We know that heaven isn't up—up above the sky. Jesus did not fly up among the clouds. Jesus in his glorified body lives like

God forever. The resurrection and the ascension are one and the same event.

But where is he?

Where are those who have gone before us—those who fell asleep in him and woke up in his likeness? Where is heaven? After all, don't bodies, even glorified ones, have to be somewhere? No, they don't.

God is everywhere—everywhere on this planet, everywhere among the stars and galaxies. All of us, all things, live and move and have their being in God. Where was God before the earth existed—before the stars and galaxies existed—before anything existed? God wasn't everywhere because there was no "where" in which to be. Before anything other than God existed, God was and God was nowhere. God was, as he is now and ever will be, but before creation God was nowhere. Even after all things came to be, God's being is not limited to the extent of the material universe. God is.

For us, "to be," we have to be "somewhere." This is the way we have to think. It's the only way we can imagine "to be," because we have minds that have to work in and through material stuff—brains of flesh that can function only in terms of space and place—in order "to be," we have to be "somewhere".   If we are nowhere, then "we ain't."

Where was God before anything existed other than God? Where was God before creation? God was nowhere, but he was. God was forever and ever, before there was space and place to be present in. We cannot imagine it, but the fact is that to be isn't the same as to be somewhere. "To be" doesn't require some "where."

Jesus lives forever in the glory of God, and where he is, there we and the whole of creation also will be, even if we cannot imagine "where." It is where that isn't "anywhere".

Do Humans Have Souls?

The description of a human being as composed of two parts, a material body and a nonmaterial—spiritual—soul, and the concept that the body dies and corrupts, but the soul continues to live, comes from Greek philosophy—and the writings of thinkers like Plato and Aristotle. According to the Judeo-Christian understanding, a human being is not a material/spiritual composite; a human being does not have a soul; a human being is a soul; a human being is a living soul; to "have: a soul means to have an identity—to have a name. Christianity took a wrong turn and came to adopt—to *baptize*—the Greek view of human nature. So, Christians prayed for the souls of the dead, and taught that at the end of time souls and bodies would once more be united in a universal resurrection.

This was a wrong turn because eternal life in the Christian Faith is not about the immortality of the soul. It is about resurrection. The promise of eternal life that Jesus taught was about the eternal life of bodily persons. We can't picture that. Just as the human mind cannot imagine what the bodily resurrection of Jesus was, so also it is impossible to picture our bodily resurrection. The caterpillar can never grasp what it means to be a butterfly, but caterpillars become butterflies. There should be a crusade to delete "soul" from the Christian vocabulary and in particular from its prayers—that is, the "Greek" soul.

Christianity is not about the salvation of souls. It is about resurrection. It is about bodily persons being raised to new life here and now and into forever, a glorious forever like Jesus. Moreover, it is about the belief that the stuff of people's lives and the stuff of material creation are the building blocks of the eternal. It is about the healing and empowering of people's lives. It is about the evolving transformation of all things into new being.

"May his soul—her soul—and the souls of all the departed through the mercy of   God rest in peace." We should pray, "May John—Susan—and all the departed through the loving power of God come to enjoy the fullness of life in him."

Some Christians have come to believe that in death the body of Mary, the mother of Jesus, by a unique privilege, did not suffer corruption, that she was assumed body and soul into eternity. In light of the understanding of Jesus's resurrection that is beyond the physical and the Judeo-Christian understanding of human nature, like the so-called ascension of Jesus, the assumption of Mary as a unique privilege doesn't really make sense.

People First Says It All

"The Sabbath was made for man" Jesus said, "not man for the Sabbath." Jesus put people first. That turned on the crowds. Some were afraid of him particularly for this. Putting people first turns everything upside down. Put people first, people as people, each and every person, their rights, needs, hopes, and dreams. In what Jesus said and did, that was his message—his vision. Let people be your focus. Let people be at your center. Let people be your glory and your joy—people, not law and order, not tradition and custom, not policy and politics, not profit and power, and not even religion. All these things have to be seen, understood, defined and applied for the good of people. It is only for people—it is only in the lives of people—that any of these things truly makes sense and has value.

Jesus was not a philosopher. To know what his message and vision were, just look at what people meant to Jesus. Look at how he loved them. What Jesus's message and vision were all about—and are all about—we find in people, in our love for one another, in our respect for one another, in our caring about one another, in recognizing that every person is made in the image of God and that each person is a daughter or son of God and a partner with God in making all things new. What matters, what is true, what is right, the world, life itself, the Bible and our Christian thinking and teaching—we have to look at it all in terms of what people should mean to us. We have to become passionate about people. The more passionate we are about people, the closer we are to what matters and the closer we are to what is true and to what is right. The more passionate we are about people, the greater and the more wonderful will be our tomorrows.

That's what Jesus was talking about—that's what he was doing. He saw people for who they were and who they could be; he saw what life should be for each person; he loved each person, person to person, and people felt their worth and knew their dignity. That's what Jesus's message and vision are all about. It's when we look at one another like that and when we love one another like that—when we put people first—that all is revealed and the lights come on, and the Spirit works and Christianity—the church—the world—can see its way and everything is made new and the realm of God comes. People first.

Let me tell you a story.

In the early 1970s I served as a program officer in the US Office of Education in Washington, DC. My responsibilities required me to visit the agency's regional offices across the country. On a trip to the federal office in Atlanta, Georgia, I asked one of our interns to accompany me. He was an African American whose family lived in the Atlanta area, and I figured it might be helpful to have him along. After we concluded our meetings at the regional office, the intern told me that since he was in the area, he was going to visit his grandmother, who lived near the Ebenezer Baptist Church, where Martin Luther King Jr. had been pastor. He asked me if I would like to go with him. The woman who lived with his grandmother was Coretta Scott King's seamstress, and we might have a chance to meet Mrs. King. The intern had told me stories about his grandmother, and yes, I wanted to spend some time with her, and it would be a privilege to meet Mrs. King.

As it turned out, his grandmother was alone. She was in her nineties; her own family had been slaves. This stately lady told some touching tales to go with our iced tea. At a point in our conversation the grandmother looked rather intently at my white face, and asked, "Are you here from your government?", and I said, "My government? Isn't it the government? Isn't it our government?" She answered, "No, it's not my government, because I don't see that the government looks at me as me. I look at you as you, and I see that you look at me as me. From the way I see it the government doesn't look at me as me, and you should know that because you look at me as me, maybe the government doesn't really look at you as you." That was a lot of years ago, and Civil rights in the USA have leaped forward since then, but her words have stayed with me. They echoed the very message and vision of Jesus, "me as me" and "you as you."

What Is Truth?

Jesus stands before Pilate. It is a very familiar scene. Pilate asks Jesus, "What is truth?" Jesus does not answer. Here is the one person who we Christians believe could answer that question, and in a way that no one else could, but Jesus says nothing. He stands there. We might imagine how Jesus could have impressed Pilate. We might wonder what Jesus's answer could have led to. Silence. Pilate waiting, looking at Jesus.

Jesus didn't answer Pilate's question because he wouldn't give Pilate the kind of answer he was expecting. Pilate wanted a definition of truth—an explanation of what truth is. Actually, Pilate asked the question sarcastically. He believed there was no such thing as truth, but he must have thought it would be interesting to hear how this teacher would try to define and explain what truth is. Jesus stood there and offered no definition and no explanation.

Jesus did not answer because the truth to which he bore witness was not to be found in definitions and explanations. Jesus was a unique kind of teacher. He was not a philosopher. He did not teach that he had the truth. Jesus claimed "I am the truth." Jesus stood silently before Pilate, and stands silent to anyone and everyone who would ask, "What is truth?" Jesus standing there was the answer. His life was what truth is. His love was what truth is. Who he was in himself, who he was for others, is what truth is. "I am the truth" because what you see in me is the way.

Jesus revealed what it means to be fully alive. Jesus revealed what love is, and how far love must go; he revealed the power of love. Jesus offered no definition and no explanation of truth. Just standing there answered Pilate's question. Just standing there answers the question for all time. His way, his life, his love were the answer—the answer that truly matters. Jesus standing there is saying, "Pilate, and anyone and everyone who has ears to hear, what you see is the truth. What you see is the truth that makes you free. What you see is the truth that re-creates you. What you see is the truth that changes the world and makes all things new." This is the truth to which Jesus bore witness.

This is the truth to which those who follow him are called to bear witness, but along the way we took some wrong turns. The truth got covered over. It got twisted up with wordy definitions and explanations. Almost from the very beginning Christians got into the business of definitions and explanations. Back in the fourth century Christians were arguing about how to define and explain who Jesus was. Was he divine? Was he human? Was he both? The argument became hot and even violent. A council of the church was called to settle the argument, and it came up with an "official" solution, and here's where the church took a wrong turn. It demanded that everyone had to accept the official solution, and anyone who did not accept it was out of the church, and no longer a Christian.

The church proclaimed that it's the official definitions and explanations that matter. These are the truth. The truth in the mind, the truth put into human words, is what makes people Christians and members of the church. As time went on, Christians got deeper into definitions and explanations. The church not only got into the business of dogmas and creeds, but these stood at the top of its product line. The truth to which Jesus bore witness, the truth to which those who followed him are called to bear witness, got rather lost in all the definitions and explanations. Tragically, this meant—and still means—that Christians continue to argue among themselves about who has the truth. This led to divisions and mayhem and outright war. Christians got into the business of judging and condemning individuals who dared to think differently as "heretics" who must be punished and even put to death.

So it is that Christians have become used to the idea that the truth to which Jesus bore witness, the truth of faith, is in definitions and explanations, in dogmas and creeds, as if the truth of faith were something of the mind—as if the truth that frees us and heals us and empowers us were set in how we think about the story of God and us, rather than in how we live the story of God and us. Of course, Christians will apply their minds to try to understand the story of God and us. After all, we can't help it; that's the way we're built. But the truth that matters, the truth that makes us free, the truth that re-creates us, the truth that changes the world and makes all things new is not in definitions and explanations, not in dogmas and creeds. The truth that matters is Jesus himself—that is, it is in the Spirit of God who dwelled in him, and who dwells within us and among us, in whom we share in the power for life and love that was in Jesus. This is the truth to which Jesus bore witness. This is the truth to which Christians are called to bear witness—the way of life and love in the very power of God.

What is truth? Truth is hope—infallible hope.

The New Ten Commandments

I. Understand that life is more than what you can count or measure.

II. Treat your fellow human beings with love, honesty and respect; respect the earth, our island home.

III. Do not overlook evil or shrink from administering justice, but always be ready to forgive wrongdoing freely admitted and sincerely regretted.

IV. Always seek to be learning something new.

V. Test all things; always check ideas against the facts, and be ready to discard even a cherished belief, if it does not conform to them.

VI. Enjoy your sex life, so long as it damages nobody else, and leaves others to enjoy theirs in private whatever their inclinations, which are none of your business.

VII. Do not discriminate or oppress on the basis of gender, sexuality, race, color or creed.

VIII. Do not indoctrinate children; teach them how to think for themselves, how to evaluate, and how to disagree.

IX. Value the future on a timetable longer than your own.

X. Live life with a sense of joy and wonder.

(Edited from *The God Delusion* by Richard Dawkins, pp. 298-299)

Jesus's Commandments

- See people and the world for what they could be.
- Open your eyes to the good you can do.
- Hunger and thirst for righteousness.
- Be merciful.
- Be pure of heart.
- Be a peacemaker.
- Love your enemies; bless those who curse you; pray for those who persecute you.
- Forgive, and you will be forgiven.
- Do not judge, and you will not be judged; do not condemn, and you will not be condemned.
- Give of yourselves, and it will be given to you, a good measure, pressed down, shaken together and running into your lap.
- Do not be angry with your sister and brother; do not insult them; call no one a fool.
- If anyone strikes you on the right cheek, turn the other also; wash one another's feet.
- Seek first the realm of God.
- Root out whatever gets in the way of your relationship with God and with one another.
- Don't be stupid; imagine what could be.

- Let your light shine in the world, and know the dignity and the responsibility of who you are, partners with God in making all things new.
- LOVE ONE ANOTHER, AS I HAVE LOVED YOU.

Sometimes when I reflect on the beatitudes, I think of Martin Luther King, Jr. The beatitudes are Jesus's "I Have a Dream" speech.

The Not-So-Golden Rule

"Love your neighbor as yourself."

"Do unto others as you would have them do unto you."

The classical, universal principle for living a moral life.

The "golden rule" that just about everybody recognizes.
Christianity signed on and adopted this rule as its own fundamental moral guideline. In light of this rule Christians critique and evaluate behavior, particularly their own, just like everybody else.

BUT…"Love your neighbor as yourself" cannot really be the Christian "golden rule." Jesus gave those who follow him a new commandment: "Love one another as I have loved you—as *I have loved you*." As time passed his new commandment faded from view, and Christians settled for the principle of loving our neighbor as ourselves, as our golden rule. Love of ourselves became the accepted measure by which we loved others. Our human capacity to love became the limit of our power to love. Moral living came to mean, and continues to mean, being fair to everyone, being respectful to everyone and hurting no one. That's not the love, and that is not the life, Jesus commanded.

He commands us to love over the top—to love totally and unconditionally. He calls us to a love that upsets everything—to a love that changes everything.

Love sinners. Love the outcast. Love those who take you for suckers. Love the down and out, even when their situation is their own fault. Love those who don't think the way you do. Love those who don't believe the way you do. Love those who don't live the way you do. Most of all, love the weak, the poor, the little guy, the stranger, the marginalized, those whom you cannot understand. Love those who persecute you. Love your enemies.

It is only when people think that our love goes too far—when even good people think our love is foolish—that we love as Jesus loved. Then love of ourselves is no longer the measure by which we love. Loving our neighbor as ourselves will not change the world. Loving our neighbor as ourselves will not make all things new. Jesus's love is our measure, and he loved without measure. Do we have the capacity to love as Jesus loved? No, we do not. He commands us to love not by our own capacity to love, but by the power of the Spirit of God, whose name is Love, who dwells within us, even as he dwelled in Jesus. He calls us to believe in the indwelling power to love—to believe in risk-taking love, to believe in self-sacrificing love, to believe in foolish love. This is the "golden rule" for those who follow Jesus, and this is the moral way that we are commanded to teach the world. This is the love that makes us believe in hope. This is the love that makes us believe that nothing is impossible with God.

Pierre Teilhard de Chardin, scientist and prophet, wrote, "Some day, after we have mastered the winds, the waves and the tides, and gravity, we shall harness the full power of love, and then for the second time in the history of the world we will have discovered fire."

New Prayer of Confession for the Episcopal Book of Common Prayer

Most merciful God, we have not loved you with our whole heart; we have not loved one another as Jesus loved us. We believe in the loving power of your Spirit who dwells within us and among us, the same Spirit who dwelled in him, and in him we place our resolve and our hope to walk in your ways. Amen.

A Circle, Not a Pyramid

When Christianity gradually took on the trappings of the declining Roman Empire, the way it understood itself was changed—it fundamentally changed its life and the understanding of its mission. In particular, it changed the role of its leaders—the clergy—and the relationship between them and the people. The clergy was raised above the people, and if Christianity can be structurally described, it changed from a circle to a pyramid. No longer were all the members of the church seen as joined hand in hand on the same level, sharing a variety of roles and responsibilities; the clergy was seen in orders above the people. Christians came to believe that the clergy was exclusively called to proclaim the "Good News"—to "feed the lambs and the sheep", and to preside at worship. The clergy came to be seen as "other Christs." The "church" came to be understood as the "clergy." "Church" and "clergy" came to be used as interchangeable terms. Further, the clergy came to be set above the people by a sacred ritual; it was numbered among the sacraments; it *conferred* spiritual powers. The ritual—ordination—changed the clergy *on the inside*, marking them with an indelible character. The clergy claimed God-given roles and responsibilities to guide, monitor, and even control the lives of the people, and even their thinking, and they taught the people to accept it all. This is "clericalism"—the clergy above the people, standing between God and them, and between them and God, and it gave birth to bureaucracy.

These fundamental changes in the Christian way result in three principal and tragic consequences. First, love, which saves and heals and empowers people and transforms the world, cannot and does not flourish; it even dies—the most stifling impact of bureaucracy. Second, growth in knowing what is true and what is good is frustrated. If only the clergy serve as agents of what is true and good, this cuts off the flow of light in the Holy Spirit, who dwells in all of us, and whose will it is to reveal truth and goodness in and through all of us, and whose will often surprises us. Third, it denies the essential roles and responsibilities of the people, who are also called by God to be "other Christs."

The clergy may have particular roles and responsibilities in the life and mission of the church. They may help ensure order and efficiency, but structurally the church is meant to be a circle, not a pyramid; the clergy is meant to stand among the people, not above them. Christianity has to understand once again its life and its mission as it did before it took on imperial trappings. Nothing could be more important in making this happen than to redefine the ordination of the clergy. This ritual does not confer spiritual powers; it does not change a person on the inside. There is nothing on the inside of a clergyperson that is any different from what is on the inside of an un-ordained person. Ordination confers authorization; it authorizes a person to function on behalf of the people, but any person has the *power* on the inside to do what an ordained person does.

As a matter of fact, any person could even be temporarily authorized by a clergyperson, or by a community, to function as an ordained person. Moreover, when we extend our belief in the universal indwelling of the Holy Spirit, that is, that the Spirit of God, dwells within and among the whole human family, it would also seem to follow that even an unbaptized person or a non-Christian could be temporarily authorized to do so. "Church" and "clergy" are not meant to be interchangeable terms, but the terms "people" (particularly, though not exclusively, the baptized) and "church" are exactly that—interchangeable.

Christianity—the church—is a circle, not a pyramid. It is a light and a force in the world to save and to heal and to empower and to make all things new, and every Christian—indeed every member of the human family—shares the privilege to make this happen, each in his or her own way.

There seems to be a common misunderstanding of religion that sounds like this. Discipline. Self-control. Live in a way that can be reasonably expected. Moderation in all things. Hold to the middle of the road. Actually, the only thing to be found in the middle of the road is mediocrity.

One of C.S. Lewis's better-known books is **The Screwtape Letters.** *It is a clever story about a master devil who teaches a young devil the most useful ways to neuter and even destroy the Christian, or any religious person for that matter. On one occasion the master devil gives the young devil this advice: "Keep whispering in the Christian's ear the need for moderation. Talk to him about moderation in all things. If you can get him to thinking that religion is all very well up to a point, and that's it, you can feel happy about that person. A moderated religion is as good for us devils as no religion at all, and certainly much more amusing."*

Christianity is not about what you have to do. It's about what you can do. It's about being everything you can be for yourself, for others, for the world and for the realm of God.

Unity—Not Creedal, Not Organizational, but Dynamic

"That all may be one."

Do Christians understand the real meaning of that prayer—that hope? Does it mean that the Christian goal is to make all Christians members of a super, worldwide church, and then to make all people Christian—all seven billion? Does it mean ultimately the conversion of all Jews, Muslims, Hindus, Buddhists and believers of every stripe to Christianity?

Before anything else what we have to understand is this. People are saved, healed, and empowered and all things are made new, not by what is in anyone's head, not by what is in anyone's creed, not by what is in anyone's traditions, and not by anything we have put together, even though much of it is reasonable and useful. People are saved, healed, and empowered, and the world is made new by the Spirit of God—by the power of the Spirit of God who abides and works within and among and through all people—all seven billion. God's work is one. God's purposes are one. God's saving, healing and empowering Spirit is one.

The real meaning of Jesus's prayer, "that all may be one" is in an all-embracing vision—that people everywhere accept his message of universal love; that everyone comes to believe that God is the With-Us-God; that everyone comes to believe that the Spirit of God, whose Name is Love, indeed abides within us and among us; that in the Spirit of God all people are daughters and sons of God and partners with God in making all things new; that everyone will live according to priorities that really matter; that all people everywhere give of themselves for one another; that everyone enjoys life in abundance; that all try to be everything they can be for themselves and for others.

This is the one flock Jesus sees and prays for—the one flock of all humanity.

This is Jesus's vision—that all humanity be one in the peace of God—that all people see that different ways to believe, to think and to live are not differences that separate people from one another; that our differences are gifts to one another, which can become pathways to a better understanding of what is true and what is good. In Jesus's vision no one can claim that his or her way is the only way; none can claim to have what is true and what is good, and the future of the human family, tied up—closed—in doctrinal packages; no one can claim exclusive authority over the works and purposes of God.

In Jesus's vision so it is that Christianity cannot be the whole of the human story. So it is that there is more to the realm of God and more to the divine-human-cosmic enterprise than the church. Christianity—the church—and any and all religion are means to an end. In Jesus's vision all believers—all people—should rejoice in the truth wherever it is found, in the good wherever it happens, in God's work and purposes wherever people recognize them, and in whatever is said and done that brings life to people, and brings it more abundantly. Jesus prayed for dynamic unity, not creedal unity, much less organizational unity.

God's work and purposes are always inclusive and never exclusive. None of this means that one point of view is as valid as another. Rather, it means that God's work and purposes, what is true and what is good, are infinitely marvelous and always beyond us. It means that the whole human family is called to live and serve together with unfailing mutual respect for one another in a never ending search to find and make our way. It means that we are called to the challenge that lies between religious authoritarianism on the one hand and religious subjectivism on the other—called to the challenge that lies between "we've got all the answers" and "nobody can have any real answers", as if there were no such thing as truth, and it didn't matter anyway. It means we are called to live and serve together in our uncertainty and with our differences, and still keep ourselves in peace. If Christians could believe like this, if they could be open like this, if they could trust like this, if they could make this dynamic unity the hope of their faith, they could enlighten the way for all peoples and all nations, and truly all things would be made more surely new.

All of this calls for much tolerance, much patience with one another and   profound humility.

This kind of humility:

My God, often we have no idea where we are going.
Often we do not see the way ahead of us.

We cannot know for certain where it will end,
nor do we really know ourselves.
The fact that we think we are on the right way,
does not mean we actually are.
We want to be, and we hope that we have that desire
in everything we are doing.
We can get lost at times, and at times seem even to walk
in the shadow of death. We will not fear,
for we have one another and you are ever with us. Amen.
(Prayer inspired by Thomas Merton)

In Jesus's vision this is the meaning of his prayer, "that all may be one".

It is more than a prayer. It is a universal challenge.

Everyone's Invited to the Table

How any part of the church views Holy Communion says something fundamental about how that part of the church understands the meaning of Jesus's vision and prayer "that all may be one." The Lord's Table should be open to the whole human family. Holy Communion is not a reward or a sign of approval for the more or less worthy. It is forgiveness and healing for the more or less unworthy; that's all of us. Holy Communion is nourishment for the hungry and the thirsty. We are all hungry and thirsty, including those who don't even realize how hungry and thirsty they are, or what they are hungry and thirsty for. Holy Communion is a sign not of a common mind and heart we already enjoy. It is a sign not of unity achieved. It is a sign of the unity we desire, the unity expected of us. It is a sign of the one Spirit who abides in us all, drawing us closer together. Holy Communion is a sign not of our wholeness; it is a sign of the health in spirit that we seek. Holy Communion is a sign not of a work completed; it is a sign of a work in progress. Holy Communion is a sign not of how we live and love here and now; it is a sign of how we want to live and to love.

There is a story about heaven that goes like this. Every morning Saint Peter found in heaven a lot of undesirable aliens, that he was certain he had never admitted. Some had not been baptized. Some were ignorant of the Bible. Many were soiled and damaged people, who as Peter saw it, had no right to be there. He decided to discover just how this leakage occurred. He prowled the ramparts of heaven, and at last he discovered a dark corner where a few stones had been removed from the wall. A crowd was creeping in. Peter rushed at them, very upset, but he was amazed to find Jesus there, helping them through the wall.

"I am sorry, Peter," Jesus said. "I know it's against the rules. These people are not all they should be. Some of them are not what could be termed orthodox in their opinions. Many of them are like the sinners I knew and associated with, but they are my friends, Peter, and I want them with me here."

Open Communion—each and every person invited to receive this Sacrament—would be a church's way of saying to people everywhere. "You are all our friends, and we want you here. One and the Same Spirit, whose Name is Love, abides in us all. Come, join us at the Table for the Meal we call Eucharist—Thanksgiving. Come and hold in your hands and taste on your lips God's embracing love for us all."

> *Something there is that doesn't love a wall…*
> *Before I built a wall I'd ask to know*
> *what I was walling in or walling out*
> *and to whom I was like to give offense…*
> *Something there is that doesn't love a wall.*
> *(Robert Frost, 1874—1963,*
> *"Mending Wall")*

A Rush of Stupiphanies

The men and women—the disciples—we meet in the Gospels appear fixed in their own ideas, stuck in their traditions. They're rather self-centered, and at times quite dense, timid, and even cowardly. They turned into giants—bold leaders, confident, competent, fearless, decisive and full of energy. They came to understand that the realm of God was within them. The life and power of God himself, the Spirit of God, dwelled within them and among them—the same life and power, the same Spirit, who dwelled in Jesus the Christ. They came to believe and to understand that this indwelling life and power made everything possible. They came to trust not in themselves, but to trust first and always in the indwelling Spirit of God, and they saw that to trust in the Spirit means to be open to wherever he leads them. They saw that they were fully empowered agents of change—worldwide change.

Christianity—the church—has to see that it is the worldwide agent of change. Everything about the church is meant to be a channel of the Spirit of God, who is the life and power for change. The "why" of Jesus has to be the "why" of the church. "See, I am making all things new," Jesus proclaims. (Revelation 21:5) Christianity—the church—has to be the community of those who seek to make all things new—to change the face of the earth. The church has to be the community of those who welcome the future.

The story of Christianity—of the church—shows that it has hardly always been the worldwide agent of change; it has often not welcomed the future; it came to be known as the agent of un-change. It preached and taught "You shall not." It taught people about their weakness, limitations and boundaries, when it should have been spreading the message of their empower-ment—the message that to be Christian means to be fully hu-man. It acted as if it had the competence and the authority to give answers, unchangeable answers, when it was more truly called to face the questions—to stir up the questions—that would challenge people and the world, and open them up to the Spirit, the power for change. It served as the worldwide *turnoff*, when it should have been the worldwide *turn-on*.

Like the first disciples, the church has to see and embrace that it is indeed the worldwide agent of change, renewal and transformation. Its focus has to be not on where it has been, but on the journey ahead—where it has to go—to focus not on its yesterdays, but on its tomorrows. Christianity—the church—has to be the sign and the confirmation of the indwelling Spirit of God, who continually dares the world to dream of things that never were and empowers Christians and the human fam-ily to make them happen.

Stupiphanies. That's what Christianity—the church—should stir up everywhere every day. What's a "stupiphany? Let's suppose you want to teach your dog to fetch. Picture it. Let's say you're in your backyard, which has a pool. Your dog is sitting there with you. You show the dog a ball, and say "Fetch." You throw the ball into the pool, point at the ball floating in the pool, and say "Fetch." The dog doesn't move. You jump into the pool, get the ball and put it on the ground in front of the dog. Again you show the ball to the dog, and say "Fetch;" you throw the ball into the pool, point to the ball, and say "Fetch." The dog doesn't move; so you jump into the pool again, get the ball, and put it in front of the dog. Again, you show the dog the ball, say "Fetch," throw it into the pool, point and say "Fetch". Still, the dog just looks at you. One more time, same thing, and again you jump into the pool, and bring the ball to the dog. Suddenly, a light dawns. This is all backward—upside down. This is not what you want. This is not the way it's supposed to go. It's not working. It looks as if the dog is smiling at you. This is stupid. You look rather stupid. You are having a "stupiphany".

What we need—what the world needs—is a rush of stupiphanies—to see things right side up—to see who we are and what life is all about, and to see who we are supposed to be, how we are supposed to act, and what we are supposed to do—to see the light—to stop being stupid—to see what our possibilities are and to know the power we have within us. That light is always shining, and Christianity—the church—is called to help us all to see everything in the clarity of that light—to multiply our stupiphanies—to fill the world with stupiphanies. If we ever pray for anything, we should pray for stupiphanies.

"Don't be stupid—imagine what could be." That's one way to sum up Jesus's message. Maybe the greatest of all mysteries and wonders, greater than all natural and man-made wonders, is deliberate human stupidity. The church—Christianity—is supposed to change all that.

No More Hungry People

Hunger is a terrible thing—not the hunger we feel because we haven't had lunch yet, but the hunger that for too many people is their way of life, each and every day. To go hungry is the most basic human indignity. People who are hungry and hardly know when they will eat again cannot know or believe anything about their true and inviolable dignity as human beings. They cannot know or believe anything about life's possibilities, about freedom or about being part of the whole human family. To those who are hungry such things can make no sense.

Our first responsibility has to be to feed the hungry, and it's about a lot more than doing our individual best for them. It's about a lot more than organizations doing what they can. It's about a radical change in our society and in the worldwide economy. It's about a vision of the whole world transformed by a radically new way of thinking and a new way of seeing things. It's about a picture of the whole world with a radically new set of priorities decided not by self-interest or politics or power, but based first and always on the dignity of each and every human being and rooted in a change of heart. It's about acknowledging that we cannot change this world of ours for the better while there are millions of people going hungry.

What is true about hunger and our physical life is also true about hunger and our life in the Spirit, but there is a difference. When people feel physically hungry, they know what that feeling is and they know what they need. They will do something about it, or at least try to do something. They will get something to eat. When people feel their spiritual hunger, quite often they do not know what that feeling is, and sometimes they don't want to know what that feeling is. People who are spiritually hungry cannot know and believe they are daughters and sons of the infinite God, partners with God in creating and transforming all things. They cannot know and believe they have a power within them that is the very Spirit of God and that the Name of this power is Total and Unconditional Love. To people who are spiritually hungry such things can make no sense. They cannot think spiritually, when going spiritually hungry is their way of life. Those of us who are more or less spiritually fed and understand what the spiritually hungry are feeling have a profound responsibility to provide them with spiritual nourishment. This is where the church comes in, or should come in.

Picture a church, and in front there is a sign displaying this message: "Welcome! We offer food and drink that can truly nourish and refresh you, food and drink that can change your life, food and drink that can change the world, food and drink that can guarantee your happiness." People are inspired by the sign, and enter the church eager for that wonderful food and drink. Again and again the food and drink they receive is not so wonderful. The food is rather under-cooked or over-cooked and not well prepared. The breads are not very tasty, and sometimes actually stale. The drinks are usually bitter or maybe much too sweet. The fruit is beautifully arranged, but it's not real fruit; it's plastic. The atmosphere is not all that pleasant, or on the other hand, rather silly. Most disappointingly of all, the church seems to be more concerned about its establishment than the hungry and thirsty people.

When spiritually hungry and thirsty people enter the church, what do they find again and again? So-called sacred texts that are meaningless or that contradict common knowledge or even common sense, unexplained or unquestionable teachings, a "one size fits all" kind of morality, traditions that are no longer applicable, exclusiveness, rules, obligations, a sense of guilt, and even judgment and censure. People are not unmindful that the church, this organized religion, is a force for good in the world around them, but too often they are not nourished at all by the food and drink they find there. So it happens that when people see that sign in front of the church, they just don't fall for it, and they pass by. But they are still hungry and thirsty.

If Christianity, the church, is going to offer food and drink that truly nourishes and refreshes, food and drink that can change people's lives and change the world, food and drink that can energize people and lift them up, then the church has to offer food and drink that is not canned, prepackaged or frozen. It's got to be fresh. More than that, Christianity—the church— has to prepare the food and drink in daring new recipes.

Like Children Standing on Their Heads

Jesus took a little child in his arms, and explained, " You see this child. You have to understand that it is to those who are like this child that the realm of God belongs." Because children ask no questions? Because children are so submissive? Because children are so accepting? Because children are seen and not heard? Anyone who believes such things about children evidently does not know them, and anyone who believes that this is what Jesus meant, doesn't know much about the realm of God. Children ask questions—why, why not and how come. Children are disruptive. Children are rebellious. Children are seen and heard, and are usually quite loud. Children are full of energy. To such as these the realm of God belongs.

The realm of God belongs to the childlike, not the childish. The childish live in their own little world, as if that's all there were. For the childish, "It's a small world after all." The childlike are fascinated with life, fascinated with the world. They're risk-takers, adventurous and open to possibilities. For the childlike, it is not a small world. It is a big world, and they are part of it, partners with God. And the bigger they know it to be, the more they see in it the infinity of the God who made it. Children are the sign of the realm of God, not because they are a sign of powerlessness, but because they are a sign of life's and the world's possibilities. "Let go," Jesus meant. Let go of your self-importance. Let go of your self-satisfaction. Let go of the gods of the marketplace. Like children standing on their heads, turn your guarantees and values topsy-turvy. The childlike are the sign of the possibilities open to those who put their trust not in themselves but in God; who put their trust not in their own *certainties*, but in the power of the Spirit of God, who dwells within them and among them. To such as these the realm of God belongs.

To make all things new—that was Jesus's mission. As children are not meant to grow up into agents of the status quo, so those to whom the realm of God belongs are agents of making all things new. To paraphrase George Bernard Shaw, "Life is no brief candle to me. It is a splendid torch which is passed to me for a moment, and I want to make it burn as brightly as possible before handing it on to those who will make it burn even more brightly after me."

The children were lined up in the cafeteria of a church elementary school. At one end of the table was a large pile of apples. A teacher posted a note on the apple tray: "Take only one. God is watching." Farther along the lunch line, at the other end of the table, was a tray of chocolate chip cookies. A child had posted a note: "Take all you want. God is watching the apples."

A Sunday school teacher asked her class to memorize the Twenty-Third Psalm. The next week she asked the students to stand, one by one, and recite the psalm. Each of the boys and girls did well, until one boy got up and began, "The Lord is my shepherd", and then nothing. Again he tried, "The Lord is my shepherd", and again and again. "The Lord is my shepherd". Finally, the teacher asked him, "Is that all you know?" The boy answered, "The Lord is my shepherd, and that's all I need to know."

Then there was Amy's prayer: "Our Father who art in heaven, how'd you know my name?"

Let me tell you a story.

It is a story of a child's faith, and a church—a community—trying to live up to its motto and goal, "to make our embrace as wide as God's".

It was a hot and humid Saturday morning in August. A team of parents was working in the school next door, doing some much needed remodeling and painting. Outside in the yard behind the school they had set up a couple of inflatable pools on the grass where their children could play while they worked inside. I was in my office and from my windows I could watch the children having a lot of fun. We had a wedding that morning, and as I got up from my desk to go to the church, I noticed that one of the little girls (let's call her Annie) had taken off her bathing suit, and began making her way from the safety of the yard toward the street in front of the school. The quickest way for me to intercept her was through the front door of the church, which also faced the street. So, I raced through the parish hall and into the church, which was already filled with wedding guests. They were treated to an extraordinary sight. Annie had not walked toward the street. Rather, when she noticed the doors of the church wide-open, she entered and processed her bare butt almost in a run up the main aisle toward the altar—wet, and rather muddy, but very much at home.. The mother of the bride, usually the last to be seated before the ceremony, was not yet in her place. So when Annie got to the head of the aisle, and saw the only empty pew, she sat down.

It would have been priceless to have a video camera, not only to film Annie's little escapade, but also the looks on the faces of the wedding guests. As I made a dash to get Annie, one of the ushers for the wedding stopped me, and asked, "Russ, do you know if this girl is groom side or bride side?" I lost it at that point and so did the guests. Laughter and some applause rocked the church. The usher had slowed down my dash across the church, and Annie was too fast for me anyway; she skipped out of the church through the parish hall and into the children's playroom. She was safe and very content. So I went over to the school to let her mother know where Annie was, and I described what had happened. She apologized over and over, but I stopped her and told her that there was no need whatsoever for any apology. Rather, I said we should celebrate the incident because if Annie felt that much at home in the church, then we must be doing something right at Saint Peter's-by-the- Sea. However, I did add that on Annie's wedding day, if I was still around, I would like very much to say "a few words" at the reception.

Back on Message—Love Wastefully

The radical reform of Christianity begins when it gets solidly back on message. God's generosity is the message. It is a message that definitely sounds too good to be true. Story after story in the Gospels carries the message, and the message is so new that it upsets all our thinking—all our logic, all of what makes sense to us. We listen to the stories. We understand the message, but it's too much. So ever since the very beginning we have turned the stories around to fit our thinking, and our logic, and what makes sense to us. Christianity can become what it is called to be, only if it turns the stories around, so that it is back on message. Maybe Jesus never actually told these stories, but they do reveal what the disciples heard and what they understood. They understood the message—they knew what the Good News was.

Let's look at some of those gospel stories.

The story of the farmer planting seed. The farmer does not carefully till the soil and mark out rows for planting. He scatters the seed everywhere. Strange. It's not at all efficient to scatter seed like that. It's foolish. It's wasteful. The story reveals the way God loves us, and it's not the way we human beings might expect. The story reveals the boundless generosity of God.

Someone came along later and offered an explanation of the story that focused on the yield of the seed—an explanation to make it fit our thinking, and our logic, and what makes sense to us. It turned the story around. It became a story not about the farmer—not about the generosity of God—but a story about the soil, about how people measure up, instead of a story about God who loves without measure.

The story of the laborers sent to work in the vineyard. Some laborers were sent into the vineyard early in the morning; some at midday; some late in the day. At the end of the day each of the workers received the same wages. That doesn't seem right. In our way of thinking that's not fair, but the story reveals that love is the new justice. It is a story not really about the laborers. It's a story about the owner of the vineyard. It's a story about generosity. It's a story that reveals the generosity of God that goes infinitely beyond anything we could imagine.

The story of the prodigal son. The young man squandered his inheritance, and in the end made his way home, tail between his legs, practicing in his mind what he would say to beg his father's forgiveness. His father overwhelmed him with his love; he had no need for words. It was a time for celebration. It is not really the story of the prodigal son. It is the story of the loving father, about his generosity—about God's generosity—so hard to believe.

Centuries before Isaiah already seemed to prophesy the message. He wrote, "Everyone who thirsts, come to the waters, and you that *have no money*, come buy and eat. Come, buy wine and milk *without money and without price*...For as the rain and the snow come down from heaven, and do not return there until they have watered the earth, making it bring forth and sprout...so shall my word be...It shall not return to me empty...It shall accomplish that which I purpose, and succeed in the thing for which I sent it...The mountains and the hills shall burst into song and all the trees of the field shall clap their hands...All of this an everlasting sign that shall not be cut off." (Isaiah 55:1—5; italics added)

Paul wrote: "The Spirit of God, who is the infinite Love of God, *the exuberant Love of God,* dwells in you...You did not receive a spirit of slavery to fall back into fear, but you have received a Spirit of adoption. When we cry 'Abba', Father—*Dad...* it is that very Spirit bearing witness—that we are children of God, and if children---*if God's daughters and sons*---then heirs of God and joint heirs with Christ." (Romans 8: 14—17; italics added)

How is it that Christianity turned the story of the sower into a story about the soil? How is it that it turned the story of the owner of the vineyard into a story about the laborers? How is it that it turned the story of the loving father into a story about the prodigal son? Jesus's message was to raise all of us to a new kind of faith in the total and unconditional love of God—faith in the wasteful love that changes us and the world. How is it that Christianity went so far off message? That's not so easy to explain, unless we acknowledge that the generosity of God sounds too good to be true, and if we believe that God is so generous with us, then we also have to be that generous with one another. To believe in the generosity of God would mean a radical transformation of the way we think and the way we feel and the way we act. We would have "to make our embrace as wide as God's." It would mean a lot of letting go. It's easier to think of our lives and our world in terms of doing the best we can, bearing what fruit we seem to be able to bear, fulfilling obligations and following the rules. That's what Christianity settled for. It took wrong turns.

No one could be unmindful of the light and love shining through the church, but this also is the way the world came to see the Faith. The church got lost among the trees of dogma and discipline, and could not see the forest very clearly.

At last it is beginning to appear that Christianity—the church—may be getting back on message, but it will take a lot of letting go to overcome what it settled for for so terribly long. The call is all the more challenging because the church's wandering among dogma and discipline has deeply infected the mind and heart of the whole human family. However mammoth the challenge, this is where the radical reform—the radical rethinking—of Christianity has to begin. It has to turn everything back around. It has to move the focus off us. It has to get back on the message of the generosity of God. God's gracious generosity establishes equality among all of us—the righteous and the not so righteous, the industrious and the not so industrious. It's not that what we do and what we don't do doesn't matter; it does. But to experience the realm of God—to experience its power and its joy--to be born again and become a new person—to change the world—we have to be alive to the generosity of God. That's the message. That's the understanding that makes—or should make—Christianity true Christianity.

A little story about my son Mike. I was tucking him in for the night. He was four years old, and had been impossible that day. I said to him, "Mike, this has not been a good day. Tomorrow will be better. Remember, just try to be good. That's all Mom and I ask of you. That's all even God expects of you. We love you, and God loves you, just for trying to be good." Mike was silent for a moment, and then he said, "You know what, Daddy? I think God loves me even when I don't try." Mike's theology was better than mine. Somehow at four years old he had already got the message.

Ephphatha

There's a story in the Gospel of Mark about Jesus healing a man's deafness. "Ephphatha'" Jesus commands, "Be opened," and the man can hear. (Mark 7: 31-37) It is more than a story about the healing of one man's deafness. "Ephphatha,"—"Be opened"—is Jesus's command to each and every one of us—to the world. "Be opened." Jesus commands us to be open to life, to growth and change, to the future, to the Spirit of God. Open up, he commands, so that we can become everything we should be, so we can see all the possibilities for ourselves and for the world.

How could anyone think he/she has the "truth" all tied up? How could anyone think he/she has the last word about what is right or what is not right? How could anyone think he/she has the questions and answers about life, our world, and tomorrow all wrapped up? What if the sciences thought that way? In particular, what if medicine thought that way? How open are we to God's story? People who think they have heard all there is to hear are deaf to God's story. They are not hearing God's story, either because it isn't being told as it should be, or because they are just not listening. Maybe they are afraid to listen, and maybe they don't want to hear what they might hear.

In Jesus's day, just like today, there were people who thought they had everything cased. "Ephphatha," Jesus taught them, and some mocked him as crazy, and some judged him dangerous, and some denounced him for blasphemy. "Ephphatha," Jesus commanded, and they crucified him. Jesus continues to teach, to command, "Ephphatha." Be open. Be open-minded. Be open-hearted. Be open to everything God's story is about. Be open to a new way of thinking. Be open to a new way of living. Be open to a new way of caring.

Be open to a new way of feeling. Be open to wherever the Spirit of God leads. "Ephphata".

We have not touched the truth and what is right until people mock us as crazy. We have not touched the truth and what is right until people judge us dangerous. We have not touched the truth and what is right until a thousand sincere people have denounced us for blasphemy. "Ephphatha."

"Merry Christmas." "Happy Lent." "Happy Easter." "Happy New Year." "The peace of the Lord be always with you." "Ephphatha." Engrave this greeting—this command—on our altars. Post it on our doors. Carry it in the deepest part of our being. "Ephphatha." "Be open." This is the most Christian of all greetings—our best wish, to one another and to the world. "Ephphatha."

Jesus Promised Joy and Laughter

I have said these things to you
so that my joy may be in you,
and that your joy may be complete.
(John 15:11)

Blessed are those who weep now,
for you will laugh. (Luke 6:21)

Jesus promised his disciples, and promises the world, joy—his joy. And more than this, Jesus promises laughter. Jesus must have been a joyful man; he must have had a great sense of humor; he must have laughed easily. So it was, that little children wanted to be close to him. The challenge of living the Faith should be full of joy, even a lot of laughs. For Christians, life is fundamentally and essentially a comedy, not a tragedy. The classical definition of a comedy is that it is a story that ends happily; a tragedy is a story that ends unhappily. No matter the conflict, divisions, injustice, disaster and setbacks of everyday life, Christians believe that the human story is a happy story because we believe that God is with us; because we believe the Spirit of God abides within us and among us, the same Spirit who dwelled in Jesus; because we believe that in the power of the Spirit of God we can and we will overcome all things; because we believe that in the power of the Spirit we can do all things, and each of us and all of us together can become everything we should be for ourselves, for others and the world; because we believe that conflict, division, injustice, disaster and daily setbacks are not of God, but that God's will for us is the fullness of life and perfect joy.

Life can be tough; it can be frustrating and depressing; it can seem impossible. But whatever we have to face, we can believe in the joy of Jesus. We can believe in the laughter of Jesus, who faced suffering and death on the cross. He promised joy and laughter, the joy and laughter that come from faith—the joy and laughter that come from knowing the God-guaranteed punch-line of every step, and of every twist and turn, in the human story and its ultimate outcome. We believe that the source of Jesus's joy and laughter was the same as ours—or better, that ours is the same as his. Joy and laughter, a solid sense of humor, are the surest signs of the presence of God. Joy and laughter are prayer that raises us up and turn on the world. Life can be a serious business; but we have had enough of the somber, and even frightening, images of Jesus the Christ. Such images, no matter how stunning and artistic, are untrue images and are contrary to the Faith. Enough of a Christianity that has been afraid of joy and laughter! It is a smiling Jesus, and it is a laughing Jesus, that reveals who Jesus is, and that's the true image of what we believe.

Let me tell you a story.

This happened in Orvieto, Italy, where I served as vicar of the Anglican/Episcopal mission. A dog had been barking for quite a while, and at first I didn't pay much attention. Two hours later the dog was still barking and it became impossible not to pay attention. I thought that maybe the dog was in some kind of distress, and I decided that I had to check it out. I didn't have to go far. Just a few steps from my apartment building I saw the dog locked in a parked car. One of the windows of the car was open a few inches, so the dog was all right, but he did not like being shut up like that for so long. I decided to look for a policeman. It was around 9:00 pm, but I figured I might spot a police car patrolling the streets. As I walked down the main street I saw a group of people up ahead, and it looked as if something was going on. I thought there might be a policeman there. Sure enough, there was a smartly uniformed member of the carabinieri—the state police. I approached him and began to tell him about the imprisoned dog. Suddenly, people were shouting out at me to get out of the way. A woman came up behind me and said, "He is not a policeman; he's an actor. We're making a film here." I had walked onto a movie set. I stepped back and watched the "policeman" play the scene. Then I spotted a couple of other policemen at the edge of the crowd. I approached them, but I asked first, "Are you actors or policemen?" They pulled my chain a bit, having seen what I had done a little while before, but they did tell me they were what they looked like. I explained about the dog, but they couldn't do anything about it. They were assigned to ensure security for the film company (a German company; the director was speaking German), and they couldn't leave their post. So back to the car and the unhappy dog—a good-sized border collie. Maybe he was hungry. I went to my apartment and grabbed some dog biscuits. I dropped them through the partly opened car window. The dog gobbled them up. No more barking. I was glad the dog seemed somewhat content, but I confess that as I walked away I thought, quite uncharitably, that maybe after eating something he might "do his business" in the car. The disgraziato who left him there deserved it. I looked out my window before I went to bed. The car was gone. I wondered if the director would keep me in the scene. My exchange with his "policeman" might make it look more authentic.

Get Rid of "Amazing Grace"

How is it that to many Christians, and most of the world, Christianity continues to be seen not so much a revelation of our human dignity, not so much a message of infallible hope, but as the distributor of universal unworthiness, weakness, guilt and fear? Why does the church, this church and that church and every church, one way or another continue to preach a message of what human beings are not, rather than who they are, and a message of what human beings cannot do instead of what they can do? Why is this the message that the missionaries carried everywhere? Why do Christians pray the prayers they pray, bewailing their wickedness and their misery? Why do Christians sing the hymns they sing? How, for instance, can they sing a hymn like "Amazing Grace," one of the most popular hymns in the Christian repertoire? "Amazing Grace, how sweet the sound, that saved a wretch like me...'Twas grace that taught my heart to fear." People can do rather wretched things, and there are times when people feel wretched about themselves, but God does not see us as wretches. God has made us all his daughters and sons, sisters and brothers of Jesus, partners with him in making all things new in the re-creation of the world, and "grace" that would teach our hearts to fear is not the grace of God.

In the Bible there are all kinds of stories about people who do wretched things, even the leading characters.

There's a story about a terribly wretched thing David did. David, the king, watched a beautiful woman taking a bath, and he was infatuated with her. He found out that her name was Bathsheba, and that she was the wife of Uriah, a military leader. But David wanted her. He sent some of the royal guard to get her, and they brought her to him. He took her to bed. She became pregnant. David figured he had to cover up what he had done, and in particular make sure Uriah did not find out. David invited Uriah to dine with him, and treated him like a poor fool. Un povero cornuto. David expected that Uriah would go home and make love to his wife, and he would think that he was the father of the coming child. However, Uriah was a noble fellow and could not bear the thought of enjoying the comforts of home, while his buddies were spending the night in the field. So, he slept in the servants' quarters of the palace. David then devised a scheme to cover up what he had done and to get Bathsheba for himself permanently. He made sure that Uriah was put into the front lines for the next day's battle. In the battle Uriah was struck down and killed. This is the story of David the rat—a Peeping Tom, an abuser of women, an adulterer, a first class liar and a murderer. It gets worse. When Joab, Uriah's commander, told David that he deeply regretted what happened in the battle—about the men who were killed, including Uriah, David told him to have no regrets, and gave Joab a high five. David was more than a rat; he was a two-faced skunk—with all due apologies to rats and skunks. David did a very wretched thing, and he must have felt like a wretch, but he repented of the very wretched thing that he did. He did not wallow in guilt and fear, because he believed first and always in the God of love, and he believed God made him in his divine image—that God made us all "a little less than the angels". Jesus would be hailed as the "Son of David," the descendent of this "non-wretch."

Then there is the story about Paul, when he was still known as Saul, and the terribly wretched things he did. When a crowd rose up and dragged Stephen, the deacon, out of Jerusalem, and stoned him to death, Saul stood there and watched. He held their coats while they did the deed, and approved their killing him. He breathed threats and murder against Jesus's disciples, and asked for letters from the temple leadership that would authorize him to arrest any men or women, who believed in Jesus, and bring them bound to Jerusalem. Wretched things. This was Saul—ruthless, arrogance personified. But he became Paul, one of the greatest non-wretches who ever lived.

God Won't Get You for That

Christianity—the church—grew into the notion that judgment and punishment for the bad things we do and for the good things we don't do is the way of things, as if judgment and punishment were the necessary way to make things right. Christians have come to accept judgment and punishment as an integral part of the fabric of the Faith. That's the way the world sees Christianity too. Christianity—the church—has to root out this notion that "God'll get you for that." Judgment and punishment are not of God. We find lots of judgment and punishment in the Bible. How much of that is of God, and how much is of the scriptural writers? It's the writers. Judgment and punishment are not God's way. That's our way. That's what the scripture writers put in the mouth of God. In this world of ours, in our lives, it is not God who punishes. Actually, we punish ourselves. When we foul up and disorder our world and our lives, it's our fouling up and our disorder that we suffer. The so-called "Ten Commandments" don't mean that if we don't do these things or do these other things, God will punish us. Rather, they are meant to caution us about fouling up our lives and disordering our world. We have to look beyond what the biblical writers wrote, and hear God saying, "I love you, and I don't want you to be unhappy. My will for you is happiness and fullness of life." We have to understand that God doesn't threaten; God doesn't punish. We punish ourselves, and then, like those ancient writers, we attribute the punishment to God. The fact is that we reap what we sow.

What about hell? First of all, we have to get rid of the images of hell that the Bible, preachers, writers and artists have given us. Hell, here or hereafter, should be defined in one word. *ME.* Not just me first. Much more than that. Only me. Life is only me. The world begins and ends with me. The only thing that matters and the only thing that can matter is me. Hell is the outcome of choosing self to the complete exclusion of everyone and everything else. Choose power, even hate—never love. Choose not to care, never caring. Choose to be self-centered, never self-giving. Choose to be unforgiving, never forgiving. Choose what breaks people apart, never what brings them closer. Choose to be uncooperative, never cooperative. Choose to be a stranger to everyone. Choose ease, never courage. Choose envy. Choose a life and a world without meaning. Choose to value only what you can count and measure. Choose dissonance over harmony, noise over melody, darkness over light. Choose discrimination, never tolerance. Choose cunning and suspicion over trust. Choose a mind and heart closed tight. Don't learn to laugh. Stay angry. Mock the peacemaker. Reject friendship. Never rejoice in the good of others. Self-sacrifice has no place in your life or in your world. See only the trees, never the forest. Hell is the dungeon of the self. Those who choose self like that are their own jailers. The doors of hell are locked from the inside. Hell burns cold, not hot.

That's hell in the here and now and what hell would be in the hereafter. We know that hell for some is real enough in the here and now. Hell in the hereafter also makes sense to a lot of believers and to theologians and preachers. Does hell in the hereafter make sense to God? God respects the freedom of each and every person. True freedom, personal freedom, makes love possible. Does the divine respect for human freedom go so far as to allow for final un-love? Is not God's Love infinitely more powerful than any and all human un-love? Is it possible for anyone to be excluded from God's embrace forever? Are not *all things* being made new in Jesus the Christ? Paul writes in his letter to Timothy, "God desires *everyone* to be saved and come to the knowledge of the truth." (1 Timothy 2:4; italics are mine.)

In the New Testament 90 percent of any mention of hell in the hereafter is in Matthew; if it were not for his Gospel, we would not be asking these kinds of questions at all. Hell in the hereafter is not mentioned in any of the creeds. The Christian faith is a positive faith. Christians believe first and always in the love of God, in the victory of God in Jesus the Christ over all the forces of un-love, the victory in which every member of the human family is called to share by the power of the Spirit of God who dwells within us all and among us all.

What about purgatory—a kind of hell with a time-line? That whole idea makes no sense at all. How could purgatory make sense to God? How could a sojourn of burning in some kind of spiritual fire make a person more worthy of the fullness of life in God? There's a lot more that we don't know than we do know about the hereafter, but we have to know that purgatory is also a rather blasphemous idea and downright ridiculous.

Christians came to accept judgment and punishment, even eternal punishment, as if judgment and punishment were of God. Christianity—the church in all its parts—has been telling this to the world for a hell of a long time. In light of the Faith, in the wisdom of the Faith, it is time to let go of this.

We Puzzle God

People, children, millions, go to sleep each night hungry, and tomorrow they will be just as hungry. Thousands upon thousands are without shelter. Thousands daily are dying of malnutrition and disease. Violence and fear are deep in the fabric of our world. Slavery comes in many forms and is still only too real. Perhaps more degrading and dangerous than anything else, the darkness of ignorance is everywhere. All this is very real, not only in some places far away, but right around the corner and up the street. Confronted with all that, we look to God. Why doesn't God, the all-powerful, the all-good God, do something about all that? Who could believe in God? Take a look around.

God looks to us, and God is puzzled. God can't really be puzzled by anything, but if God could be puzzled by something, this would be it. We say we can't figure God out. God says he can't figure us out. Why doesn't God do something about all that? He did. He made us his partners. We puzzle God. God looks to us and asks, "Why don't you do something about all that? I can't figure your priorities: profit, comfort, self-interest, bureaucracy, law and order, regulations and procedures, process and statistics, customs, traditions and creeds. You spend your resources, time and energy on everything from weapon systems to cosmetics. Your entertainment, even your games and your toys, are full of destruction and death. Your politicians refuse to legislate gun control. You foul up nature's resources. You put guts ahead of brains, fists ahead of hearts. You announce that you stand on principle, but you actually hide behind them. You are afraid of growing up. You will not think outside the box. You ask too many "whys", and you should be dreaming of "why nots". You are a puzzle. Why don't you do something—why don't you do a lot more about what confronts you? You look to me. You are looking for magic. I have not made you puppets. I am not pulling the strings. I have made you in my image. I have given you the rich and fruitful earth. I have endowed you with reason and skill. I have empowered you with my Spirit".

God asks us: Will you please help me? Will you please help me to save the world?...Please be my partners. Will you please be my collaborators? Will you please help me to change the ugliness of the world? Will you please help me to bring peace where there is war? Will you please help me to bring reconciliation where there is quarreling? Will you please help me to bring joy where there is sadness? Will you please help me to bring togetherness where there is separation? ...Will you please help me to make my children know that they are my children, that we belong together, that we will survive only together, that we will be free only together, that we will be human only together.?
(Desmond Tutu, Sermon: Saint Francis Church, Managua, Nicaragua, 1989)

Till all the jails are empty and all the bellies filled;
Till no one hurts or steals or lies, and no more blood is spilled;
Till love and race and gender no longer separate;

Till pulpit, press and politics are free of self and hate;
God has work for us to do.
(Carl P. Daw Jr, 1944— "Till All the Jails Are Empty")

When Bad Things Happen

People continue to think that when bad things happen—illness, misfortune, accidents and death, it is "God's will." One way or another, the church got people to believe that. This is a belief that really, *really*, has to be corrected. When bad things happen, it's not God's will. Illness, misfortune, accidents, and most of all, death are not God's will. Bad things are not of God, and cannot be of God. It is blasphemy to say they are of God. If bad things were God's will, then we would have to conclude that the person who lived more contrary to the will of God than anyone ever did was Jesus. Page after page of the Gospels are filled with stories of Jesus's compassion—stories of how he healed every kind of illness and turned around every kind of misfortune—stories even of his raising the dead. Bad things are not and cannot be God's will, no matter what slant or twist is given to such a belief. God's will for everyone and for the world is abundant life and complete joy, here and hereafter.

God lived a human life in Jesus to reveal his will for us and for the whole of creation; to reveal that his Spirit dwells within and among us; to reveal that in the power of his indwelling Spirit all things are possible and all things are being made new; and especially to reveal God's challenge to us to make his will real, in particular for the poor, the oppressed, the destitute, the sick, the hungry and the homeless, those in prison, the persecuted, refugees, those in sorrow or any kind of trouble and for any and all the marginalized of society

God places his will for life and joy in the hands of the human family.

A little girl dies of leukemia. Who could dare say her illness and death were God's will? The question to be asked is not why God didn't prevent it. The question has to be why we didn't prevent it. It is for the human family to discover how to prevent and cure illness. It is for the human family to upgrade life and to ensure joy. The question is how rightly and wisely does the human family make the decisions that will bring life and joy to people. Does the human family use its resources to make God's will real? How many wrong decisions have been made? How much of human resources are used in ways that are a waste of God's good gifts? Billions of dollars on more efficient ways to destroy and to kill. Billions on everything from shinier cars to tummy tucks. Then a little girl dies of a disease that the human family should have found a cure for by now, and there are people who dare to say it is God's will? Men and women return from the battlefield maimed or in boxes, and people dare to call that God's will? Does God will war? Bad things are not and can never be God's will.

Moreover, when bad things do happen, then God is especially with us. Indeed, God's will is life and joy. He challenges us to use his gifts in the power of his indwelling Spirit to make his will real, but this does take time. In the meantime we can use these same gifts to alleviate the consequences and the fallout of the bad things that continue to happen along the way.

In the end, we all face death, but God's will for us is that like Jesus, through death, we come to perfect life and perfect joy forever.

Bad things are not God's will. God's will for us is life and joy, here and hereafter.

This is the Christian way to think.

Let me tell you a story, and you will never see a fork in the same way again.

A woman had been diagnosed with cancer. It was very aggressive and advanced. She was given only a few months to live. Her doctor told her to start making preparations. So she contacted her pastor and asked him to come to her house to talk about her final wishes. She told him which hymns she would like sung at her burial service, what Bible passages she would like read, and even what she wanted to be wearing. Everything was in order, and the pastor was about to leave, when the woman added something. "There's one more thing," she said excitedly. "What's that?", the pastor asked. "This is very important," the woman said. "I want to be buried with a fork in my right hand." The pastor stood looking at the woman, not knowing quite what to say. "That shocks you, doesn't it?", the woman asked. "Well, to be honest, I am puzzled by such a request," said the pastor. The woman explained. "In all my years of attending church socials and functions, where food was involved—and let's face it, food is a big part of any church event, spiritual or otherwise—my favorite part was when whoever was clearing away the dishes of the main course would lean over and say, 'You can keep your fork.' It was my favorite part because I knew something good was coming. When they told me to keep my fork, I knew something special was about to be served. It wasn't Jell-O or pudding. It was cake or pie, something with substance. So I want people to see me there in that casket with a fork in my hand, and I want them to wonder what's with the fork. Then I want you to tell them something good is coming. So keep your fork too."

The pastor's eyes welled up with tears of joy as he hugged the woman good-bye. He knew this would be one of the last times he would see her before her death, but he also knew that the woman had a better grasp of what God has prepared for those who love him than he did. She knew, really knew, that something good was coming. At the funeral people were walking by the woman's casket and they saw the pretty dress she was wearing and the fork in her right hand. Over and over the pastor heard the question, "What's with the fork?" And again and again he smiled. In his sermon the pastor told the people about the conversation he had had with the woman shortly before she died. He told them about the fork and about what it symbolized to her. He told the people that he could not stop thinking about the fork and that they probably would not be able to stop thinking about it either.

It's About Being There and Showing Up

Woody Allen, writer/actor/director, once summed up life like this. "Eighty percent of success is showing up." Right on!

Being a friend is about being there and showing up.

Being a good citizen—a patriot—is about being there and showing up.

Being all you can be for yourself, for others and for the world is about being there and showing up.

Being a Christian is about being there and showing up.

Miracles are about being there and showing up.

A man and his wife are awakened at three o'clock in the morning by a loud knocking on their front door. The man gets up and goes to the door. A stranger is standing there in the pouring rain. "Could you please give me a push?", he asks. "Not a chance," says the husband. "It's three o'clock in the morning." He closes the door and goes back to bed. "Who was it?", asks the wife. "Just a stranger asking for a push, and I think he's been drinking." "Did you help him?" "No, I did not. It's three o'clock in the morning and it's raining hard." "Well, you have a short memory," says the wife. "Remember about two months ago? We broke down in the middle of the night after that party, and this guy showed up, and was there for you? Shouldn't you do the same?" The man throws some clothes on, goes out into the pounding rain and calls out in the dark, "Hello, hello?" "Hello," is the answer. "Do you still want a push?" "Yes, please," comes the reply from the dark. "Where are you?, asks the husband. "Over here on the swings," the stranger replies.

A young man was starting a new business, a landscaping business, and he wanted to come up with a catchy slogan to paint on the side of his truck. He considered several plays on words about gardens, and asked his mother for her suggestions. Right away she thought of how personally frustrated she got with a service company that didn't keep appointments and kept her waiting for hours, and sometimes didn't come at all. She suggested a slogan that would really catch people's attention. She told him, "Paint this on the side of your truck": "We show up!"

Life, and particularly life in the Spirit, is about being there and showing up—It's not about what we have time for; it's about what we make time for. It's not about who we are, or who we think we are; it's about what we are. It's not about where we're coming from; it's about where we're headed. It's not about what was or what might have been. It's about what can be. It's about walking the walk—walking in what we say we believe. It's about making all things new, one opportunity at a time—one corner of the world at a time.

Being there and showing up. That's what the divine-human-cosmic enterprise comes down to for us.

Christian—human—and loner are contradictory terms.

Let me tell you the story about the "Belles of Saint Peter's"
Maybe you've seen the movie Calendar Girls. *It came out in 2003. The story takes place in a town in England; a group of women, who want to raise money for the local hospital, publish a calendar with each of them featured in a tasteful pose of undress. Their effort turns out to be more successful than they could have imagined. Several women, members of Saint Peter's Church in Narragansett, Rhode Island, where I served, were inspired by the movie to do the same thing to raise money for the church's capital campaign. They decided that the women to be featured in the calendar would have to be at least seventy years old, and their costumes would reflect the month they posed for; e.g., January in New Year's Eve balloons; March in St. Patrick's Day green; April with an umbrella; June as a bride; July as the Statue of Liberty, September behind a basket of apples (basket not quite large enough); October as a Halloween witch; November serving the turkey (the bird not quite large enough), December as a gift giv-ing elf.*

Frankly, our calendar was a lot more colorful than its English prototype. The local media found out about the project; the press interviewed the women, the TV stations filmed them and me. The national media picked it up, and the calendar became a news item across the country. Orders for the calendar poured in, many with letters congratulating us for what the calendar was doing for older women everywhere—for how they felt about themselves. Our bishop was very excited about the calendar; she wanted one autographed by all the models. The calendar had to be reprinted twice. What started out as a personal parish project with rather modest goals turned into a nationwide phenomenon—they sold almost two thousand calendars and made a significant contribution to the capital campaign. More than anything else the calendar lit a fire under the congregation. All that happened almost ten years ago, and a few of these wonderful women, so full of life, have passed away. I was there at the interment of the ashes of Miss July. Just before the columbarium was sealed, her son came forward with the calendar, folded it open to July, and placed in next to the urn. Life, the life of faith, thank God, can be a lot of good fun—fun from the heart—fun that lasts.

The Quality Of Mercy Is Not Strain'd

"I don't know how I can ever forgive him for that." More than likely this means , "I don't know how I can ever forget what he did." If someone says, "I'm sorry for what I did," the response might be, "That's all right; forget it; it never happened." That's not forgiveness. That's sweeping it under the rug. Forgetting and forgiveness are two different things. Forgiveness really sounds like this: What you did really hurt. I might not forget what you did, and may not for a long time, and maybe I will never be able to forget it, but you tell me that you're sorry for what you did, and you promise that it will never happen again. You promise to make up for what you have done, and to restore what can be restored and to repair what can be repaired. You want to look forward, and that's what I want too. So I want you to know this: I wish you good, and only good, or at least I want to wish you good, and only good. You have been part of my life, and I have been part of yours. If only it could be so, and if it's not the way it was, maybe in some other way. But even if not at all, I want truly to wish you good, and only good. You and I are imperfect human beings like everybody else, and we live in an imperfect world. I know that I, too, can and will be less than I should be, and maybe a lot less. I will always need forgiveness, too, and you might very well be the one I need to forgive me.

A Christian is a person who forgives. A Christian understands that forgiveness is about much more than this or that act of forgiveness. Forgiveness is about understanding what it means to be a human being. It's about understanding, and trying to understand, what we are made of, and about who we are and who we are not yet. Forgiveness is about an attitude about life, about ourselves and others. It's about acknowledging the imperfect world we live in. Forgiveness is love and caring between and among imperfect human beings in an imperfect world. Forgiveness is about hope for ourselves, for others and for our world. Forgiveness begins with "I am sorry." It begins with regret for not being who we could be and should be, but more than anything, forgiveness looks not to yesterday and to what was. Forgiveness looks to tomorrow and to what can be.

Forgiveness says "I believe in love. I believe in the power of love to heal and to transform. I believe in the power of love to change the world—to make all things new." Forgiveness means we never give up on others, that we never give up on ourselves and that we never give up on our world. Our forgiveness, true forgiveness, reflects the forgiveness of God. God never gives up on what can be. Our forgiveness says we don't ever give up either.

"I am sorry." "I need another chance." "You had a lot of chances already." To forgive also should mean "Who's counting?" "You are forgiven." "Here's another chance, and another chance, and another chance." Forgiveness is not easy—and sometimes apparently quite impossible—but the same Spirit who dwelled in Jesus dwells in and among us, so that by his power, the power of infinite Love, we are raised up and empowered to forgive "seventy times seven times."

To be unforgiving is to be without hope, as if love, as if the very power of the Spirit of God, were not strong enough to overcome un-love in all its forms—as if love cannot heal, as if love cannot change things, as if love cannot make all things new. To forgive means to believe in the power of love—to believe in the power of the Spirit of God. When we forgive, we believe all things are possible with God.

The quality of mercy is not strain'd
It droppeth as the gentle rain from heaven
Upon the place beneath. It is twice blest.
It blesseth him that gives and him that takes.
It is an attribute of God himself.
And earthly power doth then show likest God's,
When mercy seasons justice.
Though justice is thy plea, consider this,
That in the course of justice none of us
Should see salvation. We do pray for mercy;
And that same prayer doth teach us all to render
The deeds of mercy.
(From Shakespeare's, **The Merchant of Venice.***)*

He got it. He really got it.

Peace—*Dolce Far Tutto*

Peace. We talk a lot about peace. We talk about our desire for peace probably more than anything else. We hear it everywhere, from the United Nations to beauty pageants. Peace. World peace. The Christian story begins with "Glory to God in the highest heaven, and on earth peace." Jesus is called the Prince of Peace. He came "to give light to those who sit in darkness… to guide our feet into the way of peace." Jesus promises his disciples, "Peace I leave with you; my peace I give you." Paul even sums everything up with: "It is to peace that God has called you."

In our worship we wish one another the peace of the Lord, and conclude it with a blessing: "The peace of God, which passes all understanding, keep your hearts and minds in the knowledge and love of God and of his son Jesus Christ…Go in peace."

What does peace really mean? What is the peace Jesus tells us only he can give? What do we understand about peace? Does peace merely name the time when we are not fighting one another? Does peace only name a situation in which nothing disturbs us? Does peace mean stillness—silence? We pray for our dead that they rest in peace. (Doesn't that familiar prayer sound contrary to what we believe about death as the doorway to the fullness of life?) The dictionary defines peace as calmness, quietness, tranquility. Some might like to say that peace means *dolce far niente*. Is this the peace we desire? Is this the peace we pray for and work for? Is this the peace we wish one another? Is peace an absence—a kind of vacuum—the absence of violence, the absence of anything to do, the absence of any disturbance? Are we to understand peace in terms of what isn't? Shouldn't we describe peace in terms of what is?

What is true peace—in our lives, in our community, in the church and in the world? What is the peace of the Lord? Why are the peacemakers called blessed and children of God? In a word, peace is another name for opportunity. Peace names the conditions, the circumstances, the situations in which nothing holds any of us back from becoming who we can be and should be—in which nothing holds us back from doing what we want to do and have to do. Peace means we have the opportunity— what we need—to overcome our fears. Peace means we have the opportunity to get on with life, each and every one of us. Peace names the conditions, the circumstances, the situations in which each and every person has, and is assured, what is due to him/her as a person—in which the dignity of each and every person is respected without distinction—in which all people enjoy and are assured the freedom to be themselves, the freedom to follow their hearts, the freedom to follow their dreams. Peace names the conditions, circumstances and situations in which all persons have the opportunity to become who they can be and should be—for themselves, for others, for the world and for the realm of God.

True peace is a tall order, but we Christians believe that by the power of the very Spirit of God who dwells in us and among us, the same Spirit who dwelled in Jesus the Christ, we can slowly but surely overcome all our un-love and can create the conditions, circumstances and situations that ensure justice, dignity and freedom to all. We pray for peace, not as if we should expect peace to drop upon us like manna from heaven. In our prayer we are hoping that God will stir up the power of his Spirit within us and among us, so that we ourselves, become peacemakers. True peace is the fruit of *our doing*.

In our worship our greeting "the peace of the Lord" is much more than social. We wish one another the joy of being who we are. We are saying to one another that we hope you know and experience totally your God-given dignity as a member of the human family and as a partner with God in making all things new. We are promising one another that we will speak up in whatever way we should speak up, and that we will do whatever we should do, so that together we will be peacemakers.

The dismissal at the end of our worship, "Go in peace" means much more than "See you next week." Again and again it is our commission, "Go, worship is over. Go, our service begins." This is the peace in which we take our leave. "Go, our service begins—our service of justice and love, our service to guarantee dignity, equal rights and freedom to each and every person. True peace cannot be described as *dolce far niente*. True peace means *dolce far tutto*.

The Virgin Birth and Its Terrible Consequences

One of the significant counterproductive developments in the evolution of Christianity was the doctrine of the virgin birth—the teaching that Jesus was born of a mother who was a virgin and that she remained a virgin for the rest of her life. It was terribly counterproductive that Christianity allowed and fostered the broad and lasting consequences of this doctrine on the life and mission of the church, not to mention the ripple effect it had on the whole human family. In his Gospel Matthew inaccurately translated the word for "young woman" as "virgin" in a passage from the writings of the prophet Isaiah, and that's particularly where the trouble began. Luke, also eager to describe the birth of Jesus as unique and extraordinary, accepted Matthew's mistranslation, and went further. In his description of the angel's announcement to Mary that she was to be the mother of the savior he has her saying to the angel, "I know not man"; that is, "I am a virgin."

Virgins do not give birth, and Paul, who wrote years before Matthew and Luke, simply says that Jesus was "born of a woman"; that is, born just like the rest of us. Mark gives no description of the birth of Jesus, but in his Gospel he tells us about Jesus's four brothers and his sisters. According to Mark, Mary had seven children. There are some Christians who rather gratuitously explain that they were her husband's children from his first marriage, or that they were Jesus's "cousins."

Mary, the mother of Jesus, was held in high esteem from the earliest times. The artwork in the catacombs of Rome and in the ancient churches is evidence of her place of honor among believers. As Christianity came into its own, the church began flexing its male muscles and Mary became the ideal woman, docile and cooperative. She became the New Eve. Eve was disobedient and sexual; Mary was obedient and sexless. Consequently, sex became associated with guilt; virginity and celibacy became the norm of holiness. The non-virgins and the non-celibates became second class citizens in the realm of God.

The doctrine of the virgin birth demanded a high price. The high price cannot be traced only to this doctrine, but it more than anything else drove up that price, and kept it there. Consequently, what did the so-called "fathers of the church" teach? They taught things such as this: Original sin was transmitted through sexual intercourse. While it is legitimate for married persons to have sexual intercourse, it is impossible to engage in it without sin. It would be wonderful if all offspring could come into the world virginally. Sex and any physical intimacy between married couples was prohibited on Sundays, on all feast days, through the entire season of Lent until the week after Easter, for twenty days before Pentecost and for twenty days before Christmas. Couples were counseled to refrain from relations for three days before Holy Communion, and they were warned that disregarding this counsel would put them in grave sin, and make them liable to the fires of hell. Jerome, who is perhaps best known for translating the Bible into Latin, the language of the people, for the first time, taught that only virgins and the celibate will enjoy one hundred percent of the heavenly reward; widows and widowers will enjoy sixty percent; the married will enjoy only thirty percent. This became a generally accepted idea, and in the thirteenth century, Thomas Aquinas, the "prince" of theologians, picked up on what Jerome thought, and agreed with him.

Recently, Christian leaders and people reacted strongly against the book, *The Da Vinci Code,* and then the film, primarily because the story was based on Jesus' having been married, and fathering a child. The strong reaction to such an idea came out of the hard and fearful teachings about human love that were injected into the Christian psyche—into the Christian psychological *genetic code.* " Jesus married? That's heresy! That blasphemes God!" Indeed, these terrible attitudes about sex are inbred into the whole human family. The very air we all breathe is infected with them. What if Jesus was married? What if he had children? Why would that make him any less than who Christians believe him to be? Wouldn't a married Jesus, a father of children, be more truly one of us?

Christianity has taught inspiring things about human love; the church has made marriage a sacramental rite. At the same time the church in all its parts--some more and some less—has much to repent in the matter of human love and sex, and has to ask forgiveness not only from Christians, but from the whole human family, for what its teachings have done, and continue to do, to people's lives.

What do the marriage vows mean? What do couples pledge when they take those vows? That they will be lovers for the rest of their lives. The best wish anyone could offer to a couple on their wedding day is to wish them romance—romance and the passion, warmth, joy, and even fun, that will make their life together what marriage is supposed to be. It is not children who make a marriage. Children make a family. The couple, their love and romance, makes the marriage. Society is not based on the family. Rightly, society is based on romance; the better the romance in the world, the better the world. Love really does make the world go round. Before Holy Communion a couple should not refrain from relations. On the contrary, they should enjoy their love romantically more than ever. Christians and the world have to overcome all the misguided teachings and attitudes, full of terrible thinking that degrades sexual love, that God has created and calls good. We all have to see human love and sexuality in the goodness and beauty intended by God, and esteem and honor its fleshy and sacred intimacy.

From the "Song of Solomon", a hymn to romantic love—a celebration of sexual love—in the Bible.

Let him kiss me with the kisses of his mouth. For your love is better than wine...Draw me after you; let us make haste...My beloved is to me...myrrh that lies between my breasts...Ah, you are beautiful, my love...as a lily among the brambles, so is my love among the maidens.

As an apple tree among the trees of the wood, so is my beloved among young men...He brought me to his house and his intention toward me was love...I am faint with love. O, that his left hand were under my head, and that his right hand embrace me... Upon my bed at night I sought him whom my soul loves.

How beautiful you are my love...your hair, your eyes, your lips, your mouth, your neck; your two breasts are like two fawns, twins of a gazelle, that feed among the lilies...How sweet is your love...your lips distill nectar...honey and milk are under your tongue.

My beloved is distinguished among ten thousand...his head, his hair, his eyes, his cheeks, his lips, his arms, his body, his speech...I am my beloved's, and his desire is for me.

Come, my beloved. Let us go forth into the fields...into the vineyards and see whether the vines have budded, whether the grape blossoms have opened and the pomegranates are in bloom. There I will give you my love.

Set me as a seal upon your arm; for love is strong as death; passion fierce as the grave; its flashes are flashes of fire, a raging flame.

Pure Sex

To be pure has come to mean "no sex." To be impure has also come to mean "to have sex"; even so-called legitimate sex suffers that meaning. When it comes to human thoughts, words, desires and action, pure and impure have come to be understood rather exclusively in a sexual sense. This pushes the long-standing idea that there is something "dirty" about sex---something less than worthy of what it means to be human. A simple syllogism shows how wrong-headed and downright foolish that is.

God created humans as sexual beings.

But, sexual thoughts, words, desires and action are dirty and less than worthy of what it means to be human.

Ergo, God created something dirty and unworthy!

Clearly, we need to take back the definitions of pure and impure.

Pure gold is gold that is only gold; it contains no admixture of other elements. Gold that does contain other elements is not pure; it is impure gold. Let's apply that definition of pure to ourselves. A pure person is a person who thinks, speaks, has desires and acts according to human nature—according to what it means to be human. An impure person is a person who is less than true to his/her human nature—the person's thoughts, words, desires and actions contain elements that are contrary to what it means to be human. When is a person impure—less than human—untrue to what it means to be human? Answer: when a person is unloving, hateful, unjust, uncaring, self-centered, close-minded, prejudiced, intolerant, violent, dark, afraid of the future, *or sexually active in a way that is disrespectful or harmful to others.* Less than truly human sexual activity is only one item on a rather hefty list of activities that are impure—less than worthy of us. To be pure means trying to be everything people should be for themselves, for others and for the world around them, and to be impure means being less than that— maybe a lot less than that.

Actually then, sexual activity that is true to what it means to be human is pure. Pure and sex are not a contradiction in terms. Having great sex that is loving or caring or expresses personal commitment or for pleasure that does a person good and harms no one in any way is perfectly human. Therefore, it is not and cannot be understood as impure, or less than worthy of us, and certainly it is not dirty. We can go further. The greater the sex, and the more imaginative and satisfying it is in keeping with what it means to be human, and the better the outcome for the person, *the more pure the person is.*

When a person is trying to be everything that it means to be human with a firm commitment and with no duplicity, no divided loyalties and no hesitation, that's what it means to be pure of heart. To be pure of heart has nothing to do with sex. According to the Gospel of Mark (Mark 6:3), Jesus had at least six brothers and sisters, so Mary, his mother, whom Christians for centuries have called "pure," must have been plenty sexual. If Christians call her pure, let it be not because she was sexless, but because they believe her to have been an extraordinary example of what it means to be human—because she believed—because she was loving, caring, selfless, respectful, tolerant, full of peace and light and open to all possibilities with God.

If and when we take back the definition of what it means to be pure and impure—to give them the meaning that applies first and always to the human heart and mind and life, rather than to the human genitals, we will have come a long way at last toward redeeming the terrible and tragic damage that Christianity—the church—has inflicted on people's lives and on the world in the name of *purity.*

Let's Hear It for Same-Sex Marriage

In the human story one and the same Spirit moves forward the things of religion and the things of the world. It is all one enterprise. As society slowly but surely is moved to legalize same-sex marriage because of its concern for universal equality before the law, so the church must bless same-sex marriage because it is called to follow the Spirit wherever he leads us.

What makes a marriage "marriage" is not something physiological or biological. It is psychological; it is spiritual. To define marriage fundamentally in physical and physiological terms reduces marriage to the animal level; it denigrates the dignity of marriage. What makes a marriage "marriage" is not the matching of a vagina and a penis. Human beings are members of the animal kingdom, but what makes marriage marriage has to be something specifically human. What makes marriage marriage is a deliberate act of mind and will; it is a personal commitment, and hopefully, ideally, a commitment in love.

In the Jewish tradition marriage is a term used to describe God's relationship with his people. In the Christian tradition marriage is used to describe the relationship between Christ and the church. If a matching vagina and penis were the sine qua non of the definition of marriage, such a biblical and theological use of the term would not be at all appropriate. It is appropriate because marriage fundamentally and essentially means a commitment of mind and will.

A simple syllogism:

A deliberate act of mind and will—a personal commitment—makes a marriage. But, two women or two men can make such a commitment to each other. Ergo, a same-sex marriage is a true and valid marriage.

Same-sex marriage is an extension of the ways that marriage is already predicated of diverse personal commitments and relationships. Marriage is clearly not a univocal term. A univocal term always means entirely the same thing in each and every predication. Marriage is an analogical term. An analogical term has a meaning that is partly the same and partly different in its predication. For example, God exists; a man exists; a dog exists; a tree exists; a rock exists. Existence—being—is predicated of God, a man, a dog, a tree and a rock not univocally, but analogically. (Existence—being—is not an equivocal term, the same term used with an entirely different meaning in its predication.) Marriage is predicated of personal commitments and relationships that are partly the same and partly different—analogically.

Marriage is predicated of the commitment and relationship of a young couple never married before; the commitment and relationship of an older couple never married before; the commitment and relationship of a young couple, one or both of whom have been married before; the commitment and relationship of an older couple, one or both of whom have been married before; the commitment and relationship of a young couple who can have children; the commitment and relationship of a young couple who cannot have children; the commitment and relationship of an older couple who can no longer have children; the commitment and relationship even of a couple who vow to live virginally (a nod to those who accept the virginal marriage of Mary and Joseph, the parents of Jesus, as fact). In each of these predications it is the mind and will of the persons involved that make the marriage, and while the situation is partly the same and partly different, no one questions whether it is a valid predication. Clearly, we acknowledge that physiology and biology do not define marriage.

Those who oppose same-sex marriage appear to want to predicate marriage univocally—that is, as the commitment of a woman and a man who can have children, and who look forward to 2.5 children, a three-bedroom house and a station wagon in the garage. Such a univocal predication of marriage is completely contrary to the diverse and very real pictures of marital commitments and relationships. (There may be some who might be willing to predicate marriage equivocally of same-sex commitments, only because the term would be the same, but it would be understood to have a meaning that is entirely different from a true marriage.)

The point is this" when we understand marriage to be an analogical predication of personal commitments, then why not same-sex marriage? (Some might want to insist that traditional marriage is nevertheless the primary analogue.") Actually, given the opportunities for adopting children and the medical possibilities for birthing children, a lesbian or gay couple could have a marriage which fits the more traditional picture of 2.5 children, a three bedroom house and a station wagon in the garage.

There are those who object to same-sex marriage because it appears to them that it vitiates their own heterosexual marriage. On the contrary, to extricate the definition of marriage from the physiological and the biological level, the animal level, enhances the dignity of marriage by focusing on what truly makes a marriage a "marriage," a specifically human and spiritual decision and act. Indeed, the more we understand what truly makes a marriage a marriage, the more seriously couples might take their consideration of marriage, which perhaps will cut down the rate of divorce.

Same-sex marriage may take some getting used to in society and in the church, but since the Spirit of God has moved us—and continues to move us—to this, another step in human evolution, then we can believe he will also provide the getting used to it.

Celebrate the Challenge of Science

Religious truth is different from scientific truth.

Its purpose is not to convey scientific information but to transform hearts. We...believe that the timeless truths of the Bible and the discoveries of modern science may comfortably coexist. We believe that the theory of evolution is a foundational scientific truth, one that has stood up to rigorous scrutiny and upon which much of human knowledge and achievement rests. To reject this truth or to treat it as "one theory among others" is to deliberately embrace scientific ignorance and transmit such ignorance to our children. We believe that among God's good gifts are human minds capable of critical thought and that the failure to fully employ this gift is a rejection of the will of our Creator. To argue that God's loving plan of salvation for humanity precludes the full employment of the God-given faculty of reason is to attempt to limit God, an act of hubris... We ask that science remain science and that religion remain religion, two very different but complementary, forms of truth. ("Clergy Letter Project"; Dr. Michael Zimmerman, Vice President/Provost, Evergreen State College)

There is no contradiction between valid science and informed religion. No one should ever have to choose between science and faith. So, for example, even from the very beginning there were Christian thinkers who did not take the biblical story of creation literally, and they even proposed that living things developed—evolved—over long periods of time. Origen, way back in the third century, for example, wrote that to take the story of creation in the Bible literally was "absurd." He questioned how there could be light and dark before the sun, moon and stars existed; how there could be plants before the sun existed; how it could have happened that God took a daily stroll in the Garden of Eden; and God couldn't find Adam and Eve, when they hid themselves.

To look for science in the Bible is like looking for the recipe for eggplant alla parmigiana in a book on economics.

The relation of religion and science and technology is going to get ever more challenging. How religion and science and technology relate to each other is all-important to the future of the human story. Evolution is not only the core component of human knowledge, as the above statement affirms. Evolution is the very key to the mind and heart of God. Evolution is the key to understanding what being human means and the key to understanding what being Christian means. The challenge that evolution offers to the Christian faith is profoundly more significant and more fundamental than the question of how human beings came to be. It requires and demands a radical reexamination, reconception and redirection of the traditional teachings of Christianity and the church.

Christians have to embrace and celebrate the challenge of science and technology, and what faith and science together can contribute to our understanding of God's creation, particularly to our understanding of the earth, our island home. Those who fear the challenge—who fear the advancement of knowledge—limit their faith to a God and to a human story way too small. Christians have to embrace and celebrate the joining together of religion and science and technology in the divine-human-cosmic enterprise.

People should come to know Pierre Teilhard de Chardin, Christians in particular. They should come to understand the kind of thinking and the vision he represents. He is a true prophet for our times. The more this kind of thinking and this vision come to be known, the more people come to understand this vision, the more faithful Christians can be to their calling to be everything they can be for themselves, for others, for the world and for the realm of God.

Pierre Teilhard de Chardin was born in Auvergne, France, in 1881, lived for many years in China, and died in Central Park, New York City on Easter Sunday, 1955. He was a geologist, an anthropologist, a theologian, a philosopher and a poet. He was also a Roman Catholic priest of the Jesuit order; and is buried on the property of what used to be a Jesuit seminary in upstate New York.

Teilhard summed up what he prophesied when he wrote: "The future of the earth, as of religion, seems to me to depend on the awakening of our faith in the future." For him, the real division among people is between those who welcome the future and those who fear it.

Teilhard's vision: Creation is not a phenomenon in the distant past. Creation continues here and now, and God has entrusted the continuing creation and the transformation of all things—making all things new—to the human family. We are involved in an enterprise of cosmic proportions in which the material stuff of creation becomes the building blocks of an eternal reality, which is the everlasting realm of God. In this enterprise matter and spirit, time and eternity are being made one until they are one forever. As the enterprise moves forward, it simultaneously gathers creation and people together until all things and the human family are brought into one, and God will be all in all. We are all agents of this enterprise—not by our own power, but in the power of the Spirit of God, who is infinite Love, the same Spirit who dwelled in Jesus the Christ, and dwells in us and among us. Love is the energy of creation and its transformation.

All people are agents of this enterprise, those who name it for Jesus the Christ and those who give it another name and those who do not name it at all. The individual dignity of every person is raised, and material creation in its every part has intrinsic and undeniable value. The sciences, technology, medicine, philosophy, arts, statesmanship and religion are partners in this one and the same enterprise. For Christians, the resurrection, the raising of the man Jesus by the power of the Spirit of God, is the sign and the guarantee of our empowerment in the Spirit. It is the sign and the guarantee of the enterprise. The guarantee of the resurrection of Jesus is not a Pollyanna guarantee. The enemies of the divine-human-cosmic enterprise, evil, which is un-love, are real—injustice, disease and disaster. The cross went before the resurrection, and so it is that in this enterprise, moving forward and gathering together have to overcome the very real, ongoing breaking down and burning out. Whatever the challenge, in the eons of time ahead, love wins out. For Christians, the resurrection, the union of matter and spirit, of time and eternity, he who now lives like God, is the image of what is happening here and now and the image of the ultimate Omega of the enterprise.

From Teilhard's writings:

"In very truth it is God, and God alone, whose Spirit stirs up the whole mass of the universe in ferment...I bless you, Matter, and I acclaim you, not as the moralizing preachers depict you---debased, disfigured---a mass of brute forces and base appetites---but as you are in your totality and true nature...Jesus, I love you, as this world which has captivated my heart, and it is you that my brothers and sisters, even those who do not believe, sense and seek through the magic immensities of the Cosmos...To say that Christ is the term and motive force of evolution, to say that he manifests himself as evolver is implicitly to recognize that he becomes attainable in and through the whole process of evolution...The world must have a God; but our concept of God must be extended as the dimensions of our world are extended...All the communions of all people, present, past and future, are one communion... Never again, please God, may we be able to say of religion that its influence has made us more indolent, more unenterprising, less human; never again may its attitude lie open to the damning suspicion that it seeks to replace science by theology, effort by prayer, battle by resignation, and that its dogmas may well debase the value of the world by limiting in advance the scope of inquiry and the sphere of energy. Never again, I pray, may anyone dare to complain of religion that it is afraid of anything that moves and thinks...One might say that a hitherto unknown form of religion---one that no one could as yet have imagined or described---is burgeoning in our hearts, from a seed sown by the idea of evolution...Far from being shaken in my faith by such a revolution, it is with irrepressible hope that I welcome the inevitable rise of this new mysticism and anticipate its equally inevitable triumph."

Evolution—that all things came to be through a process of gradual development—on the one hand appears impossible, and at the same time is a fact. Evolution appears impossible because it contradicts the very nature of material things. By their nature material things tend toward breaking down and burning out, not building up. Mountains and shorelines erode. Living things age and die. We may say that we are not getting older, we are getting better, but we know better than that. The evidence says otherwise. Yet on the other hand, there is all the mounting evidence that things have proceeded step-by-step. As material creation got older, it did get better. Living things became more complex and more refined, more perfected. Evolution points to the future that can be and will be, even against the experience that says it cannot be. There is a power, a positive, dynamic force, in material creation that moves it forward despite itself. Christians call that power, that force, God. Evolution, once a dirty word for believers, carries within it evidence for the existence of God.

Hope appears impossible, and at the same time hope is a fact. Even from the very beginning of the human story, human experience is stacked against hope: selfishness, division, conflict, deceit, betrayal, injustice, un-love and hate. Yet on the other hand there is all the evidence that we are moving forward, slowly perhaps, even too slowly, two steps forward and one step back, but the human story is making sense and is moving forward. Christians believe that despite ourselves the Spirit of God within us and among us guarantees it. The doomsayers are wrong. The contrary forces of decay and death in nature are not winning, and neither are the contrary forces in the human story. To be Christian is to believe in the future. The most un-Christian thing is not to believe in the future—the future of material creation and the future of the human story—one future. The power, the force, within material creation, and the power and force within the human story, are one and the same, God himself. Whatever the signs of decay and death, whatever the dark and the cold, God guarantees the future for all things and for the whole human family, a future evolving, proceeding, maturing and reaching into eternity.

Five Things Not Up for Grabs

Are there things that are absolutely true? Things that are not open to question? Things that cannot change? Things that cannot allow for any exceptions whatsoever? Are there "absolutes"? People have to answer this question for themselves, as they see things. For me, there are absolutes, and there are five. I accept some things with varying degrees of open-ended certainty, but I accept these five things as absolutely certain.

- Life, the world, the human story have meaning.
  There is a "why" to it all. We are not a chance happening of nature. The human story is not merely a series of episodes and challenges. It is all part of an evolving divine-human-cosmic enterprise. Human beings, individually and together, are responsible for the directions and the outcomes of the enterprise.
- The human mind can and does know objective truth.
  Truth is "what is"—"what is so." We can reach for and we can know—we can connect with—"what is" and "what is so." Other epistemologies affirm that the human mind can only organize and categorize sense perceptions and observations, and cannot have any knowledge of—cannot connect with—things and events in themselves. On

the contrary, in and through sense experience the human mind can and does know "what is" and "what is so"—human knowledge is not limited to organizing and categorizing our sense experience. The human mind can and does go beyond sense experience, and can and does know and understand things and events in themselves—objective truth.

The human mind also can and does know objective good. Good is "what ought to be" and "what ought to be done." These are not merely categories of the mind. The mind can and does evaluate objects and behaviors in themselves—objective good.

- A human being is a free and self-responsible person.

  We are more than a machine. We are more than the result of positive and negative conditioning, conscious or subconscious. Human beings are more than the sum of their parts. We are animals, but eminently more than that. We are persons with a unique dignity and with unique identities. We have free will. We can love. We are self-determining, not as self-determining as we think we are, but neither are we as predetermined as physiologists, psychologists, psychiatrists or behaviorists think. Our personhood, our capacities for self-determinations, mean we are meant to become everything we can become and do everything we can do to the fullest extent of our individual potential for our own good, the good of others, and for the good of the world.

- God exists.

  God is infinite and eternal. God is the Ground of all being. God's name is Love.

- Jesus of Nazareth, who was crucified and died on the cross, is gloriously alive; he lives like God.

For me, the Bible can *not* be the Word of God. God can *not* be triune. Christianity as a religion—the church—can be entirely a human invention. Religious doctrines, philosophical thought, and scientific positions and theories can be debunked one after another. I could live with all that.

On the other hand, for me, life and the world and the human story cannot *not* have meaning; we human beings *cannot* be imprisoned within our senses so that we have to be satisfied with only a subjective knowledge of truth and goodness; human freedom and self-determination *cannot* be an illusion; human beings cannot *not* be more than highly developed animals or fleshy, finely programmed robots; God cannot *not* exist and God's Name cannot *not* be Love; and Jesus's death on the cross *cannot* have been the end of him.

Funny thing about absolutes. You cannot prove them.

Anti-Semitism is Blasphemy

I have visited the site of what was a Nazi concentration camp near Dachau, a town outside Munich, Germany, an enclave of suffering and death for thousands of Jews—men, women and children, husbands and fathers, wives and mothers, sweethearts, teenagers and little ones, even the littlest. The camps, like the one at Dachau, have been cleaned up, cosmetically speaking. My visit was not long after World War II, years before any makeover. There have been few tragedies in the human story—if any—that even begin to reveal the power of evil like the persecution of the Jews of Europe and the world not so long ago. I visited Dachau on a gray, overcast, chilly mid-August day that felt more like November. There were the stark barracks, and inside I saw the scratched messages on the cement walls— terrified and terrifying—messages. I entered the gas chambers where stripped naked, herded and huddling together, they died. There were the ovens where the bodies of the dead, and the not quite dead, were burned. I saw large hooks on beams above the ovens where the bodies hung like so much meat. I knelt at the mass graves inscribed with the numbers of unidentified victims who were buried there. I thought of the wisdom, talent and genius, love and laughter, art and skill that were lost to the human family in camps like this.

All prejudice is wrong—intrinsically and always wrong. That horror was prejudice in the extreme—blindness and hate at their worst. It is also wrong and blind and hateful for Christianity not to see and not to confess that that horror was rooted in its own sins. Prejudice and persecution of the Jewish people were integral parts of the Christian mind-set almost from the beginning. It is not enough to condemn the past. Formal declarations about the relationship between Christians and Jews fall far short. Anti-Semitism is still very real. The lethal poison of prejudice and persecution was there in the horror we must not forget, but also here, evidenced not only so obviously by violence and deliberate stupidity, but also by our *innocent sins*—the innuendos, the stereotyping, the remarks, and even the jokes, that continue to contaminate the human story. For a Christian any anti-Semitism—any hint of it—is not only wrong. It is blasphemy.

Jesus was a Jew. He looked like a Jew. He thought and talked and acted like a Jew. He was at home with being Jewish. To be Christian is to believe that it is in Jesus the Jew, in his life and in his death, that the total and unconditional love of God is revealed. To be Christian is to believe that in raising Jesus the Jew from death, the indwelling presence and the work of the Spirit of God are confirmed to the world. To be Christian is to believe that Jesus the Jew is the Cosmic Christ—the Omega Point of the divine-human-cosmic enterprise. To be Christian is to believe that in our Eucharistic worship it is in the self-giving of Jesus the Jew that we share, and in Holy Communion we are spiritually healed and nourished by Jesus the Jew. To be Christian is to believe that Jesus is our Jewish brother. Mary, his mother, blessed among women, is the Jewish mother par excellence. To be Christian is to relate to the Jews as uniquely our sisters and brothers. Peter, Paul and the rest are the Jews—the foundation upon which the church is built.   Anti-Semitism for us as Christians is a contradiction of our Faith and a denial of our own identity.

> *My soul magnifies the Lord,*
> *and my spirit rejoices in God my Savior...*
> *He has helped his servant Israel,*
> *in remembrance of his mercy,*
> *according to the promise he made to our ancestors,*
> *to Abraham and to his descendants forever.*
> *(Song of Mary, Luke 1:46-55)*

Episcopalians on the Crest of the Waves

We Episcopalians—and Anglicans worldwide—must find ourselves in the vanguard—on the front lines—of the reform of Christianity and the church universal. We must trust not in ourselves, nor in our own wisdom, but in the Spirit of God, whose name is Love, and who is with us every step of the way.

We have to reform our worship, our Prayer Book, our Hymnal, our structure, and our polity. We have to lead the way in answering Jesus's call to make love the new justice—to put people first. We have to lead the way in affirming more than ever that none of us has been appointed judge over another, that no one can make an exclusive claim to what is true or what is good. We have to lead the way in showing that the differences among Christians are not reasons for separation and division; rather these are gifts to one another in our common and united commitment to make all things new. We have to lead the way in our common effort to re-focus the Faith.

We Episcopalians—like all Anglicans—believe that often things are not so clearly black and white, but also that things are never gray. We believe that the Christian way—Jesus's way—shines always with all the colors of the rainbow, reflecting his fullness, the fullness of which we have all received. We Episcopalians are not *relativists*—not rudderless. We believe that what is true and what is good are always infinitely more than we could ever wrap up in our own packages. We would not dare think that what we think is necessarily what God *thinks,* just because we think it is. That's humility. That's reverence. That's "fear of the Lord," which is the beginning of wisdom. We believe that to be Christian—to follow Jesus—is to make our embrace as wide as God's. In our questions, in our doubt and uncertainty, in our confusion and conflict, and in our insecurity, whatever our differences, we must believe that Love is our infallible guide. That's not relativism. That's faith. Our assurance along the way is in Jesus's new commandment that we love one another as he loved us.

There are those who describe the Episcopal Church, and the whole Anglican Communion of Churches, as *pandemonium.* It is *Holy Pandemonium.* It is an awesome adventure in the Spirit, and we have to become more adventurous than ever.

"I believe God through Christ in the Holy Spirit blesses the Episcopal Church to be one small but shining hope that the vision of what a real, living Christian Community can be is not a dream but a reality. As Jesus taught over and over again the purpose of the Gospel is to bring people together through faith to love and to serve. Consequently, he repeatedly welcomed the most ragtag, disparate, contentious, antithetical, confused, zealous, conservative, radical collection of persons he could assemble. He calls them his friends. He made them into a community, holding them together with no bonds stronger than love.

We are still the motley crew of Christ. We are still men and women of a thousand different opinions who are called to live together in spite of ourselves. We are the volunteers in God's experiment called community---in the experiment called the Episcopal Church." (Steven Charleston, retired Episcopal bishop of Alaska)

The Business of America Is People

Let me wave the Stars and Stripes.

The opening words of our Declaration of Independence:

"We hold these truths to be self-evident, that all men [and indeed women] are created equal, that they are endowed by their Creator with certain inalienable Rights, that among these are Life, Liberty and the pursuit of Happiness."

The preamble of the American Constitution:

"We, the People of the United States, in Order to form a more perfect Union, establish Justice, insure domestic Tranquility, provide for the common defense, promote the general Welfare, and secure the Blessings of Liberty to ourselves and our Posterity do ordain and establish this Constitution of the United States of America."

There is a prophetic call in the documents of America's birth—the call to justice, the call to equal opportunity and freedom for all. America was born out of a prophetic vision. America was to be an adventure in the human spirit. America was born out of hope and a commitment to turn things upside down. On October 18, 1781, as Lord Cornwallis surrendered his sword to George Washington at Yorktown, the British fife and drum corps played a tune, an appropriate tune, "The World Turned Upside Down."

Americans respond:
"We pledge allegiance to the flag of the United States of America, and to the Republic for which it stands, one nation under God, indivisible, with liberty and justice for all."

One nation under God? President Calvin Coolidge is *credited* for affirming that "the business of America is business." First of all, "under God" has to mean we don't believe that. "Under God" has to mean we believe that the business of America is people, and not only the people of America, but the people of the world. Under God has to mean we believe we have to do everything we can to bring people together, to narrow the gap between the "haves" and the "have nots," that we believe we must be a nation that cares for its own people and for people everywhere. "Under God" must mean that we believe that the most un-American thing we could ever do would be to exclude anyone from our dream for ourselves and for the whole human family.

America! Right or wrong! No! Never! "Under God" cannot mean that we believe in America, whatever it does and whatever it does not do, as if we must assume that America is always in the right—as if we must assume that God is always on our side." Under God" must mean that we believe the responsibility of each and every American is to help ensure that America is truly in the right—as President Abraham Lincoln said, to make sure America is on God's side. "Under God" must mean that we believe we are part of the family of nations, each nation and all nations together sharing in the bounty of the earth, our island home. The Stars and Stripes! Americans' hearts should leap at the sight of our flag because it represents America's commitment to universal justice, to caring for the whole human family and to peace—true peace founded in justice and caring, that as a nation we are proud to be part of.

Each and every American is called to the role of prophet, but we have to understand that it is not for prophets to tell people how to think; it is for prophets to encourage and urge people *to think.* It is not for prophets to tell people how to care, but *to care.* It is not for prophets to tell people what to say or how to speak, but to stir up people *to have something to say and to speak up and speak out.* It is for prophets to inspire people to see that the more questions they ask, the more faithful they are to their calling, because when they ask questions they are looking to what can be and should be, and will not settle for what is, much less for what was. It is for prophets to help people understand what patriotism really means. Patriotism and nationalism are two very different things. Nationalism turns us in on ourselves; it means a surrender to yesterday. Patriotism opens us up to the vision and the hope that gave America birth; it means a commitment to today and tomorrow.

America is not a Christian nation. The Declaration of Independence and the Constitution did not give the United States a Christian birth. These documents are meant to manifest America's partnership with the nations of the world in the human enterprise—and, if you will, in the divine-human-cosmic enterprise. We Americans, with our sisters and brothers of a diversity of religious traditions and with those of no religion, have to understand and accept our role as prophets, and as patriots, and faithful to the vision and hope of our birth, commit ourselves to what can yet be for America and for the world.

Afterword

What I offer in these essays, I realize, is really *too far out* to some. The church, in all the churches, has done a great job in getting people to buy what it advertises, and it means a lot to a lot of people. So, if what you find in these pages upsets you, hurts you, or disturbs your peace, I am very sorry, but I think it's time, my friends—it's time to let go.

I am a Christian in the Episcopal Church, but I confess that at worship I can no longer say the Creed. I cannot say I believe, that I give myself , that I give my heart , to philosophical definitions and to the images and literal interpretations of stories that are not the Faith, but only the packaging of the Faith. I believe that we are still in the age of early Christianity, and the day will come when the followers of Jesus will grow into a new kind of Creed, a dynamic Creed, that expresses faith in the empowering God, who is Love, and in the divine-human-cosmic enterprise. It will be a Creed that is not a Creed at all. It will be a Declaration of Commitment to the things that can be and will be, and to all the possibilities that God has entrusted to the human family and to the future that reaches into eternity.

Some may think that what I have come to believe and not to believe is hardly in keeping with the Christian Faith. I believe I am a faithful Christian. I understand that there are those who might judge me as faithful no longer. They might be right that I am no longer faithful to the way things are with Christianity and in the church, but I believe I am being faithful to where things point—to where the Spirit is leading us. It's time to let go.

A man tumbles over the edge of a cliff, and as he falls he grabs hold of a tree branch jutting out from the side of the cliff. Holding on for dear life, he looks up to heaven and prays. "Save me. Save me." A voice out of heaven reassures him, and then tells the man, "First, let go of the branch." The man asks, "Is there anybody else up there I could talk to?"

My friends, there is no one else up there. That's the voice of the Spirit of God.

It's time, and more than time, to let go.

Declaration of Commitment

We believe in God, the Infinite Love, in whom all things came to be and evolve, the God of this planet Earth, our island home, and its myriad of peoples and cultures, who is God of the eons of time past and yet to come and of the galaxies and what else may be out there among the stars.

We believe in Jesus the Christ, in whom God is uniquely known and experienced, and in his New Commandment that we love one another as he loved us. In his suffering and death the loving power of God, with whom all things are possible, was perfectly revealed. And through his death Jesus began to live like God.

We believe that in the life and death and glory of Jesus the revelation of the purpose and the meaning, the direction and the destiny, of the human family and of all things is confirmed.

We believe that God, who dwelled in Jesus, dwells in every person—to heal us, to make us whole, and to empower us to become everything we can be and stand as partners with God and with one another in the divine-human-cosmic enterprise to make all things new. In his loving power we will be faithful to our partnership with him and with one another.

We believe in the church, the Community of Light and Love, which calls us to make our embrace as wide as God's and inspires us and challenges us to grow into our full stature as human beings.

We believe that like Jesus through our death we will enjoy the fullness of life in God. We believe that the stories of our lives, our struggles and our success, our hopes and our dreams, and the stuff and the forces of the material universe are the building blocks of the eternal reality to come when God will be all in all.

AMEN.

Made in the USA
Lexington, KY
23 August 2013